10754995

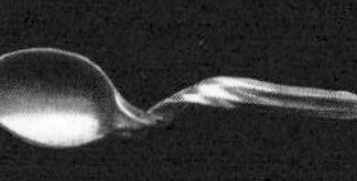

THE FOLDED CLOCK

GERHARD RÜHM

THE FOLDED CLOCK

100 number poems

translated from the german by

ALEXANDER BOOTH

TWISTED SPOON PRESS

PRAGUE

2025

ISBN: 978-80-88628-11-8

This publication was supported by a grant from the Federal Ministry for Housing, Arts, Culture, Media and Sport of the Republic of Austria.

Federal Ministry
Housing, Arts, Culture,
Media and Sport
Republic of Austria

CONTENTS

dedicated to my wife, monika, who passed in 2023

a recounting

a note on recitation

at first the "m" should barely be audible, then slowly intensified over a long stretch of time until it feels like a whimper being produced by a piercing, bodily pressure you can only resist with the last of your strength (meanwhile the "m" will have become a purely squeezed sound) – then the sound will briefly be recognizable again as "m" before the "eins!" bursts forth from your wide-open mouth (think of giving birth); this is all to be done in a single breath, so that the tension also comes from physical exertion until the liberating ejaculation of the "eins!" can no longer be prolonged.

each further "mmm-eins" varies somewhat in intensity and is no longer geared toward gradual preparation and length-of-breath but articulated with an increased level of effort, yet waning strength in a desperate struggle against the growing realization of how hopeless it is to insist on your own standards. each new number should be pronounced as if it had just been invented and placed in the room.

ascending numerals should be spoken with more and more intensity and culminate with an exclamation mark; descending numerals, on the contrary, more softly; in terms of volume, descending numerals should also be spoken a few levels lower. anything mechanical is to be avoided, nothing should appear rehearsed – and yet, nothing should appear unsure or without tension.

even with the occasional dip or treading-of-water, keep in mind that all speech together with the ever-increasing crescendos are to rise throughout the text to the point of the ad nauseam "a myriad!!!!!!"

mmmmmmmmmmmmmmmmmmmmmmmmmmmmmm mm-eins!
(brief pause)

two!
one two. –
one two – three!
    two
one two three – four!
    two
one two three four – five! –
        three
one two three four five – six!
        three
one   six, seven!
                   five
              four
        three
    two
one
    two   four   six –   eight!!
              four   six   eight!
                            seven eight
    two   four   six seven eight
                        six   eight – – nine!
                            seven
                   five
        three
one
    two   four   six   eight – nine – ten!
one two three four five six seven eight nine ten
one two three four five six seven eight nine ten – – – eleven!!
one
one
one

one
one
one
one
one
one
one
eleven!
ten, eleven!
ten, eleven!
nine – ten – eleven
nine – ten – eleven
–
nine – ten – eleven!
eight nine ten eleven
eleven?
–
two four six eight ten! – – – twelve!
eleven twelve!
ten
eight
four
six
two
four six eight ten twelve
ten eleven twelve
nine ten eleven? twelve??
three
three six
three three six twelve –
three
three
thir-teen!
thir-teen

four-teen
fif-teen
sixteen
seventeen eighteen nineteen – twen-ty!
–
twenty-one
twenty-two twenty-three twenty-four
twenty-five twenty-six twenty-seven twenty-
eight twenty-nine thirty!
ten – – twenty – – thirty!
forty!
fifty!!
sixty
seventy eighty – ninety – –

ten, twenty, thirty, forty, fifty – –
fifty! – – – hun-dred!!!
(brief pause)

(starting again very quietly, but only as a memory of the beginning:) mmmmmmmmmmmmmmmmmmmmmmm-eins!
(uniformly, almost apathetically, as if to yourself:)
one
one
one
(etc. – 100 times total, the last 10 "ones" rising in strength and intensity until:) one-hundred-one!
two-hundred!

(somewhat more decisively:)
mmmmmmmmmmmmmmmmmmmmmmm-eins!! – – –
three-hundred
four-hundred
five-hundred

six-hundred
seven-hundred
eight-hundred
nine-hundred – – –
– – – thou-sand!!! –
mmmmmmmmeins!!!

one-hundred
two-hundred
one-thousand-five-hundred,
two-thousand
four- six- eight- ten-thousand!
fifty-thousand!
one-hundred-thousand!
a mill-ion!!!
mmmmm-mm-m-eins(!!!)

one-hundred-million!
nine-hundred-million!! – – –
a thousand mill-ion!!!!
mmmmmm-mmm-m-mm-eins(!!!)

a billion!!

a thousand billion!!!
trillion!!
a thousand trillion!!
quadrillion!! quintillion! sextillion! septillion! octillion! – – –
non--plus-ultra!
(with the last of your strength, whimpering, all-atremble, voice breaking and failing:)
mmmmeins(!!!!)

(stretched into a roar:)
: : : a my-ri-ad!!!!!!

(as if in a trance, more enraptured with every line:)
myriad
myriad myriad
myriad myriad myriad
myriadmyriadmyriadmyriad
myriadmyriadmyriadmyriadmyriad
myriadmyriadmyriadmyriadmyriadmyriad
myriadmyriadmyriadmyriadmyriadmyriadmyriad
myriadm (abruptly cover your mouth with a hand)

101. a number poem

1 1 2 1 2 3 1 2 3 4 1 2 3 4 5 1 2 3 4 5 6 7 8 9
10 9 10 19 8 7 6 5 4 3 2 4 6 8 10 12 14 16 18 19
18 20 19 20 21 23 25 27 29 30 29 31 30 31 32 34
36 38 40 38 39 40 40 38 37 35 33 31 30 29 27 25
23 21 19 18 20 22 21 19 17 15 13 11 9 7 5 3 1 2
3 4 5 6 7 8 9 10 20 30 40 50 51 60 62 70 74 80
88 90 99 100 50 1 10 1 5 1 3 1 2 1 3 2 1 2 1 2 3
2 1 2 4 3 2 1 2 3 4 2 1 2 3 4 5 6 7 8 9 10 1 9 1
2 3 4 5 6 7 8 9 10 11 10 9 8 7 6 5 4 3 2 1 12 1
13 2 14 3 15 4 16 5 17 8 19 20 10 1 12 21 32 23
14 5 10 20 35 40 60 80 85 86 87 88 89 78 67 56 45
34 23 12 1 2 1 3 1 4 1 5 1 6 1 67 78 89 90 10 100
11 100 99 1 2 100 1 91 2 80 3 70 4 60 5 54 6 43
7 32 5 21 3 2 1 2 3 4 2 1 2 4 6 5 3 1 7 5 3 1 2
3 5 8 13 21 34 55 89 98 99 100 99 2 1 2 4 6 8 10
20 40 60 80 99 100 21 31 41 51 61 71 81 91 100 99
100 98 99 100 91 92 93 94 95 96 97 98 98 99 99
100 99 100 8 6 4 2 99 100 99 100 9 7 5 3 1 99 100
98 99 99 100 99 99 9 10 19 20 2 4 6 8 9 7 5 3 2
4 3 1 4 6 5 1 6 8 7 8 1 9 10 11 2 4 6 8 3 5 7 9
4 6 8 10 5 7 9 11 12 10 8 6 13 11 9 7 15 13 11 9
10 12 14 16 17 15 13 11 12 14 16 18 19 17 15 13
14 16 15 17 16 18 17 19 20 22 23 21 22 24 25 23
24 26 28 25 27 29 30 28 26 24 22 21 23 25 27 29
30 31 30 31 32 34 36 38 39 37 35 33 32 34 33 35
49 47 45 43 44 46 45 47 46 48 47 48 49 50 48 46
51 49 47 52 50 48 49 50 51 52 53 52 53 54 53 54
55 56 57 58 59 60 61 62 63 64 65 64 65 66 65 66
67 68 67 68 69 70 71 70 72 71 73 72 74 73 75 74
76 78 75 77 79 81 83 85 87 89 90 92 94 96 98 99
98 96 94 92 90 88 86 84 82 80 88 98 92 94 96 98
99 97 95 93 91 92 94 96 98 99 100 96 98 100 97 99
97 95 93 94 96 98 100 99 97 95 93 91 89 90 92 94
96 98 100 99 97 95 93 91 92 93 94 95 96 97 98 99
100 99 100 100 99 88 77 66 55 44 33 22 11 9 7 5
3 2 1 4 6 8 10 5 1 4 3 2 1 2 1 3 2 1 2 1 2 1 1 1
2 3 4 5 6 7 8 9 10 11 12 13 14 15 16 17 18 19 20
30 40 50 60 70 80 90 100 99 100 80 90 45 50 60 80
40 70 45 50 60 30 15 14 29 30 60 90 9 8 7 6 5 10
15 30 60 100 1 2 3 4 5 10 20 40 70 69 68 67 66 65
60 99 61 100 62 100 63 1 2 4 8 16 32 64 3 2 1 100

60 30 15 1 100 50 100 60 100 70 80 40 20 10 5 1
2 1 12 1 13 1 14 1 15 30 1 20 30 60 6 66 5 66 4
77 3 80 90 2 100 1 20 1 19 2 18 3 17 4 16 5 14 6
15 7 16 8 19 100 1 99 2 98 3 97 4 96 5 95 6 94 7
93 8 92 9 91 1 80 2 79 3 78 4 77 5 76 6 75 7 74
8 73 9 72 10 71 11 70 12 70 13 69 14 68 15 67 16
66 17 66 16 65 17 64 18 63 19 62 20 61 21 60 22
59 23 58 24 57 25 56 26 55 27 56 26 55 27 55 28
27 28 54 29 53 30 52 31 51 32 52 33 52 34 51 35
50 36 49 37 48 38 47 39 46 40 45 41 44 42 43 44
45 46 47 48 49 50 51 50 51 51 50 51 50 49 48 47
46 45 44 43 42 41 40 39 38 37 36 35 34 33 32 31
30 29 28 27 26 25 24 23 22 21 20 19 18 17 16 15
14 13 12 11 10 9 8 7 6 5 4 3 2 1 1 1 1 1 1 1 1 1
1 1 1 1 1 1 1 1 1 1 1 1 1 1 1 1 1 1 1 1 1 1 1 1
1 1 1 1 1 1 1 1 1 1 1 1 1 1 1 1 1 51 50 52 50
51 52 52 52 50 53 53 53 53 50 54 54 54 54 54 50
55 55 55 55 55 55 50 56 56 56 56 56 56 56 50 57
57 57 57 57 57 57 57 50 58 58 58 58 58 58 58 58
58 50 59 59 59 59 59 59 59 59 59 59 10 9 8 7 6 5
4 3 2 1 2 2 3 3 4 4 4 4 5 5 5 5 5 6 6 6 6 6 6 7
7 7 7 7 7 7 8 8 8 8 8 8 8 8 9 9 9 9 9 9 9 9 9 10
10 10 10 10 10 10 10 10 10 11 11 12 11 13 11 14
11 15 16 61 62 26 73 37 28 82 91 20 19 28 82 93
39 40 4 45 9 90 99 89 98 17 8 7 87 78 79 97 16 96
69 70 7 17 69 95 14 41 55 10 11 12 13 94 93 12 11
92 91 10 19 20 21 11 22 44 55 10 11 22 33 44 88
89 99 18 19 20 22 21 20 3 24 20 40 80 44 88 97 16
7 70 77 14 55 66 67 70 6 5 4 3 4 3 2 1 7 1 8 9
10 1 11 2 1 12 3 2 1 32 21 3 5 3 2 1 4 3 2 43 54
3 2 1 65 4 3 2 1 76 54 3 2 1 87 65 4 3 2 1 98 76
5 4 3 2 1 99 87 65 43 21 32 43 54 65 76 87 98 99
100 1 2 100 12 34 56 78 99 100 12 23 34 45 9 8 7
6 5 4 3 2 1 23 45 67 89 18 9 8 17 18 9 8 7 6 5 4
3 2 1 12 3 15 6 5 4 9 8 7 6 15 4 32 1 23 5 4 9 8
7 6 5 43 21 64 10 9 8 7 6 5 4 3 2 5 4 3 2 1 2 3
5 8 13 21 34 55 66 77 88 99 100 9 8 7 6 5 4 3 2
1 2 3 4 5 6 7 8 9 10 11 12 13 14 15 16 17 18 19
20 21 22 23 24 25 26 27 28 29 30 31 32 33 34 35
36 37 38 39 40 41 42 43 44 45 46 47 48 49 50 51
52 53 54 55 56 57 58 59 60 61 62 63 64 65 66 67

68 69 70 71 72 73 74 75 76 77 78 79 80 81 82 83
84 85 86 87 88 89 90 91 92 93 94 95 96 97 98 99
100 10 1 50 100 55 4 3 2 51 61 71 81 91 100 10 1
99 100 98 99 100 97 98 97 98 99 100 19 9 10 99 10
11 100 91 100 10 91 100 90 91 92 93 94 95 96 97
98 99 100 95 96 97 98 99 96 97 98 97 98 99 98 99
99 100 99 100 99 99 100 99 99 99 100 100 99 99 99
99 99 99 99 99 99 100 10 100 11 9 1 99 100 50 4 3
2 1 91 1 92 1 1 93 1 1 1 94 1 1 1 1 95 1 1 1 1 1
96 1 1 1 1 1 1 97 1 1 1 1 1 1 1 98 1 1 1 1 1 1 1
1 90 100 99 100 2 99 100 1 100 1 1 100 1 1 1 100
1 1 1 1 100 1 1 1 1 1 100 1 1 1 1 1 1 100 1 1 1 1
1 1 1 100 1 1 1 1 1 1 1 1 100 1 1 1 1 1 1 1 1 1
100 1 1 1 1 1 1 1 1 1 1 100 1 1 1 1 1 1 1 1 1 1 1
100 99 18 9 8 7 6 5 4 3 2 1 2 3 4 5 6 7 8 7 6 5
4 3 2 1 2 3 4 5 6 [illegible] 6 5 4 3 2 1 2 3 4 5 [illegible] 5 4
3 2 1 2 3 4 [illegible] 4 3 2 1 2 3 [illegible] 3 2 1 2 [illegible] 2 1 [illegible]1 [illegible]

12! a number poem

a note on recitation
to be spoken aloud in an animated and very rhythmic way, with particular emphasis given to underlined numbers

3, 4,
1 2 3
2 2 3
3 2 3
4 2 3
5, 6,
1, 2 and 3
2, 2 and 3
3, 2 and 3
1 2 3 4
1 2 3 4
5 and 6
5 and 6
5 and 6
5 and 6
5 and 7
5 and 9
6 and 9
7 and 9
8 and 9
9 and 9
10 9 8 7 6 5 4 3
2, 1,
2, 1,
2, 1,
3 2 1
4 2 1
5 2 1
6

7
8
9
1 2 3
1 2 3
4
1 2 3 4
1 2 3 4
1 2 3 4
1 2 3 4
2 3 4
3 4 5
4 5 6
7, 8 and 9
8, 9 and 10
9, 10 and 11
10 11 1
9 11 1
8 11 1
7 10 2
6 9 3
5 8 4
5 7 4
5 6 4
5 5 4
5 5 5
1 2 3 and 4
1 2 3 and 4
1 2 3 and 4
1 2 and 3 4
1 and 2 and 3
1 and 2 and 3
1 and 2 and 3
1 and 2 and 3 and 4 and 5 6
1 2 3 4 5 6
1 2 3 4 5 6
7, 8

1 3 5 7
2 4 6 8
1 3 5 7
2 4 6 8
1
2
1
2
1
2 and
1
2 and
1 and 2 and 3 and 4 and 5 6 7 8
1 – 9
1 – 9
1 – 9
1 – 9
1 – 9
1 – 9
1 – 9
1 – 9
1 – 9
10 – 9
11 – 9
10 – 11
1
2 .
3 . .
4 . . .
5 . . . .
6 . . . . .
7 . . . . . .
8 . . . .
9 . . . .
10 . . . .
11 . . . .
12!

the same in rhythmic notation

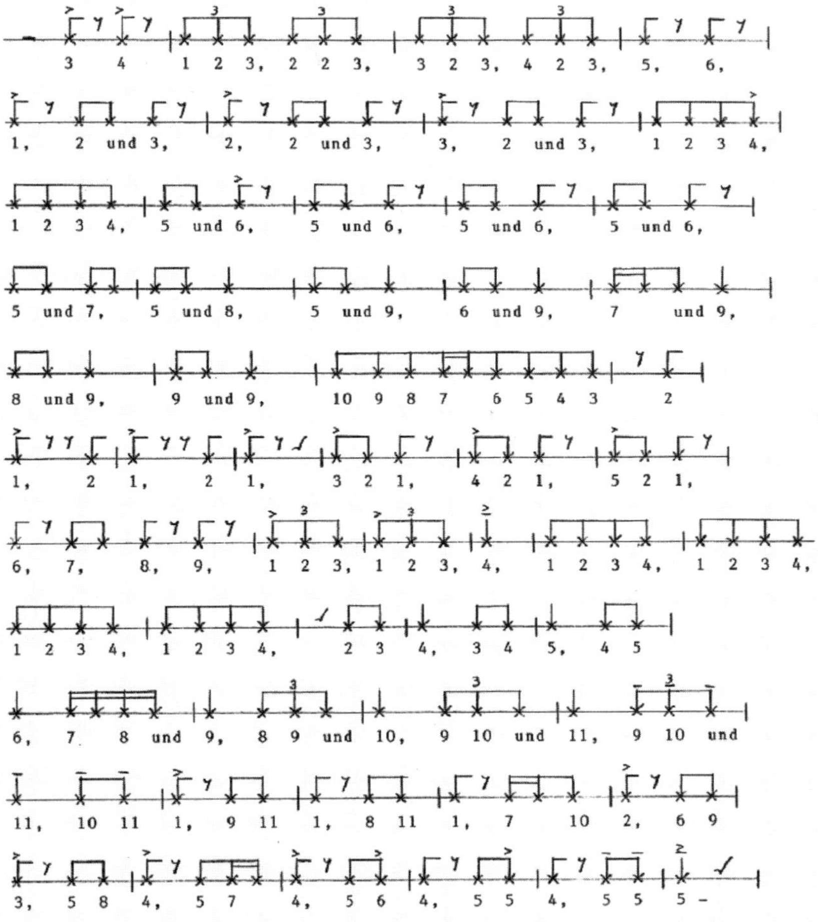

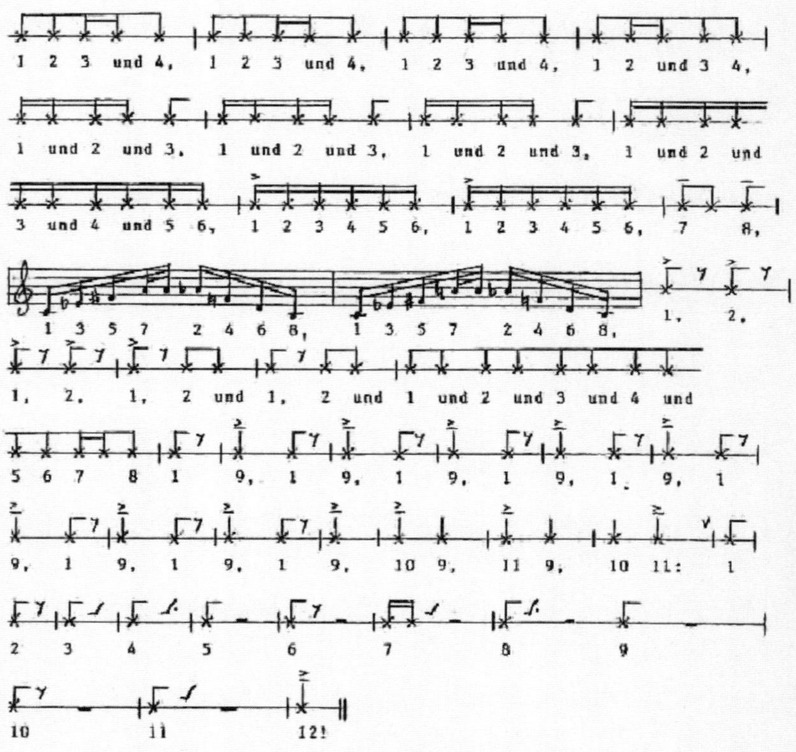
1 2 3 und 4, 1 2 3 und 4, 1 2 3 und 4, 1 2 und 3 4,
1 und 2 und 3, 1 und 2 und 3, 1 und 2 und 3, 1 und 2 und
3 und 4 und 5 6, 1 2 3 4 5 6, 1 2 3 4 5 6, 7 8,
1 3 5 7 2 4 6 8, 1 3 5 7 2 4 6 8, 1, 2.
1, 2. 1, 2 und 1, 2 und 1 und 2 und 3 und 4 und
5 6 7 8 1 9, 1 9, 1 9, 1 9, 1 9, 1
9, 1 9, 1 9, 1 9, 10 9, 11 9, 10 11: 1
2 3 4 5 6 7 8 9
10 11 12!

time poem

a note on recitation

recited in real time, the "time poem" would take an entire year: were you to begin on january 1st, you would recite only a single line a day until december 31st, then, on that day, a single line an hour until one p.m. then every half hour until, beginning at 11:30 p.m., one line every minute and, beginning at 11:59 p.m., one line every second. in effect, this could probably only be realized as a long-term event or in private. at a public recital, the intervals, if to be made clear, would have to be distinguished from one another in stages: starting from a minimum of one second, the seconds would have to last one second each, the minutes two seconds, the half-hours three, the hours four, and, last but not least, the days five or six (always calculated from the end of one line to the next). employing this model, it would take more than thirty minutes. the most practicable solution, of course, would simply be to recite all the lines in one continuous sequence.

1 january, 12 a.m. : bang!
2
3
4
5
6
7
8
9
10
11
12
13
14

15
16
17
18
19
20
21
22
23
24
25
26
27
28
29
30
31
1 february
2
3
4
5
6
7
8
9
10
11
12
13
14
15
16
17
18
19

20
21
22
23
24
25
26
27
28
1 march
2
3
4
5
6
7
8
9
10
11
12
13
14
15
16
17
18
19
20
21
22
23
24
25
26
27

28
29
30
31
1 april
2
3
4
5
6
7
8
9
10
11
12
13
14
15
16
17
18
19
20
21
22
23
24
25
26
27
28
29
30
1 may : the milky way forms
2

3
4
5
6
7
8
9
10
11
12
13
14
15
16
17
18
19
20
21
22
23
24
25
26
27
28
29
30
31
1 june
2
3
4
5
6
7

8
9
10
11
12
13
14
15
16
17
18
19
20
21
22
23
24
25
26
27
28
29
30
1 july
2
3
4
5
6
7
8
9
10
11
12
13

14
15
16
17
18
19
20
21
22
23
24
25
26
27
28
29
30
31
1 august
2
3
4
5
6
7
8
9
10
11
12
13
14
15
16
17
18

19
20
21
22
23
24
25
26
27
28
29
30
31
1 september
2
3
4
5
6
7
8
9 : the solar system comes into being
10
11
12
13
14 : the earth forms
15
16
17
18
19
20
21
22
23

24
25 : life germinates
26
27
28
29
30
1 october
2
3
4
5
6
7
8
9
10
11
12
13
14
15
16
17
18
19
20
21
22
23
24
25
26
27
28
29

30
31
1 november : continues
2
3
4
5
6
7
8
9
10
11
12
13
14
15
16
17
18
19
20
21
22
23
24
25
26
27
28
29
30
1 december : atmospheric oxygen
2
3
4

5
6
7
8
9
10
11
12
13
14
15
16
17
18
19 : fish begin to swim in water
20
21
22
23
24 : sauria crawl ashore
25
26
27 : birds fly through the air
28 : the sauria die out
29 : primates appear
30
31 12 a.m.
1 a.m.
2 a.m.
3 a.m.
4 a.m.
5 a.m.
6 a.m.
7 a.m.
8 a.m.
9 a.m.

10 a.m.
11 a.m.
12 p.m.
1:30 p.m. : appearance of ramapithecus, our distant ancestor
2:00 p.m.
2:30 p.m.
3:00 p.m.
3:30 p.m.
4:00 p.m.
4:30 p.m.
5:00 p.m.
5:30 p.m.
6:00 p.m.
6:30 p.m.
7:00 p.m.
7:30 p.m.
8:00 p.m.
8:30 p.m.
9:00 p.m.
9:30 p.m.
10:00 p.m.
10:30 p.m. : the first humans struggle to survive
11:00 p.m.
11:30 p.m.
31
32
33
34
35
36
37
38
39
40
41
42

43
44
45
46 : light a fire
47
48
49
50
51
52
53
54
55
56
57
58
59 minutes, 0 seconds : paint cave walls
1
2
3
4
5
6
7
8
9
10
11
12
13
14
15
16
17
18
19

20 : practice agriculture
21
22
23
24
25
26
27
28
29
30
31
32
33
34
35 : build cities
36
37
38
39
40
41
42
43
44
45
46
47
48
49
50 : sumerian and egyptian culture
51 : the alphabet
52
53
54
55

56 : dawn of new era
57
58
59 : humans land on the moon

a numerical constellation

½   22
4444
  333
½   5
5555

a proportional poem

4
22
24
42

equitable equation

4 + 4 = 8
8 + 8 = 4

change of position

```
1 3 5 7 9
        6 8
          4 2 0
              0
              0
              0
              0
              0
              0
              0
              0
1             0
```

basic mystical equation

1 + 1 = 1
1 + 2 = 1
1 + 3 = 1
1 + 4 = 1
1 + 5 = 1
1 + 6 = 1
1 + 7 = 1
1 + 8 = 1
1 + 9 = 1
9 + 8 + 7 + 6 + 5 + 4 + 3 + 2 +1 = 0

dreamt equation

four-and-twenty and
five-and-forty
          is
one hundred-six-and-forty

from inside to outside to inside

a counting text

1
2
3
4
5
6
7
8
9
10
9
8
7
6
.
4
3
2
1
2
3
4
.
.
7
8
9
10
9
.
7
.
.

4
3
2
1
2
.
4
.
.
7
.
9
10
.
.
7
.
.
4
.
2
1
2
.
.
.
.
7
.
.
10
.
.
.
.
.
.
.

2
1
.
.
.
.
.
.
.
.
10
.
.
.
.
.
.
.
1
.
.
.
.
.
.
.
.
.
.
.
.
.
.
.
.
.
1

digits and letters

1
2
3
4
5
6
7
8
9
one
2
3
4
5
6
7
8
9
one
a second
3
4
5
6
7
8
9
one
a second
a third
4
5
6

7
8
9
one
a second
a third
a fourth
5
6
7
8
9
one
a second
a third
a fourth
a fifth
6
7
8
9
one
a second
a third
a fourth
a fifth
a sixth
7
8
9
one
a second
a third

a fourth
a fifth
a sixth
a seventh
8
9
one
a second
a third
a fourth
a fifth
a sixth
a seventh
an eighth
9
one
a second
a third
a fourth
a fifth
a sixth
a seventh
an eighth
and the ninth

verses

8 n u g e
r 3 b ä
g e k 8 7
n r r n

ä 0 7 s
n r g k 8
n u e 1 6
e n e n

lucky calculation 2006

76 67
13 13
4 4
8
4
2

seven doubled signs

..(„oo=8“):

burials

a hamburg number poem

5 00 92 11

intersection

00
00
00
00
00
00
00
00
00
1 2 3 4 5 6 7 8 9 10 11 12 13 14 15 16 17 18 19
20
30
40
50
60
70
80
90
100
110
120
130
140
150
160
170
180
190

homage à kurt schwitters

A
B
C
D
E
F
G
H
I
J
K
L
M
N
1 2 3 4 5 6 7 8 9 10 11 12 13 14 15 16 17 18 19 20 21 22 23 24 25 26
P
Q
R
S
T
U
V
W
X
Y
Z

1
2
3
4
5
6
7
8
9
1 2 3 4 5 6 7 8 9 10 11 12 13 14 15 16 17 18 19 20 21 22 23 24 25 26 27 28 29 30
20
30
40
50
60
70
80
90
100
200
300
400
500
600
700
800
900
1000
2000
3000
4000
5000
6000
7000
8000
9000
10000
20000
30000
40000
50000
60000
70000
80000
90000
100000
200000
300000
400000
500000
600000
700000
800000
900000
1000000
2000000
3000000
4000000
5000000
6000000
7000000
8000000
9000000
10000000
20000000
30000000
40000000
50000000
60000000

0000006
00000007
000000008
0000000009
00000000001
0000000009
000000008
00000007
0000006
000005
00004
0003
002
01
0
10
200
3000
40000
500000
6000000
70000000
800000000
9000000000
10000000000
9000000000
800000000
70000000
6000000
500000
40000
3000
200
10
0
01
002
0003
00004
000005
0000006
00000007
000000008
0000000009
00000000001
0000000009
000000008
00000007
0000006
000005
00004
0003
002
01
0
10
200
3000
40000
500000
6000000
70000000
800000000
9000000000
10000000000
9000000000
800000000
70000000
6000000

1111111111ʟ1111111111
1111111111ʟ1111111111
1111111111ʟ1111111111
1111111111ʟ1111111111
1111111111ʟ1111111111
ʟʟʟʟʟʟʟʟʟʟʟʟʟʟʟʟʟʟʟʟʟ
1111111111ʟ1111111111
1111111111ʟ1111111111
1111111111ʟ1111111111
1111111111ʟ1111111111
1111111111ʟ1111111111

1 . . . .
1 2 . . . .
1 2 3 . . . . . .
1 2 3 4 . . . . .
1 2 3 4 5 . . . .
1 2 3 4 5 6 . . .
1 2 3 4 5 6 7 . .
1 2 3 4 5 6 7 8 .
1 2 3 4 5 6 7 8 9
. 2 3 4 5 6 7 8 9
. . 3 4 5 6 7 8 9
. . . 4 5 6 7 8 9
. . . . 5 6 7 8 9
. . . . . 6 7 8 9
. . . . . . 7 8 9
. . . . 8 9
. . . . 9
. . . . 8 9
. . . . . . 7 8 9
. . . . . 6 7 8 9
. . . . 5 6 7 8 9
. . . 4 5 6 7 8 9
. . 3 4 5 6 7 8 9
. 2 3 4 5 6 7 8 9
1 2 3 4 5 6 7 8 9
1 2 3 4 5 6 7 8 .
1 2 3 4 5 6 7 . .
1 2 3 4 5 6 . . .
1 2 3 4 5 . . . .
1 2 3 4 . . . . .
1 2 3 . . . . . .
1 2 . . . .
1 . . . .

unification litany

firstly : 1
the only
one of
one's
number one
the first
one of the first
the first of one
on one hand
one part
the first to come first
for the first
once more
one to one
one at a time
every 1
every 10th
every 100th
every 1000th
1 million
in any event united
to be one
one and all
all one
alone
all minus one
or by one more?
it comes down to one thing
one and the same
one way or another

one day
1st floor
10th floor
100th floor
1000th floor
for now

6 x 6 number poem with piano

a materialization

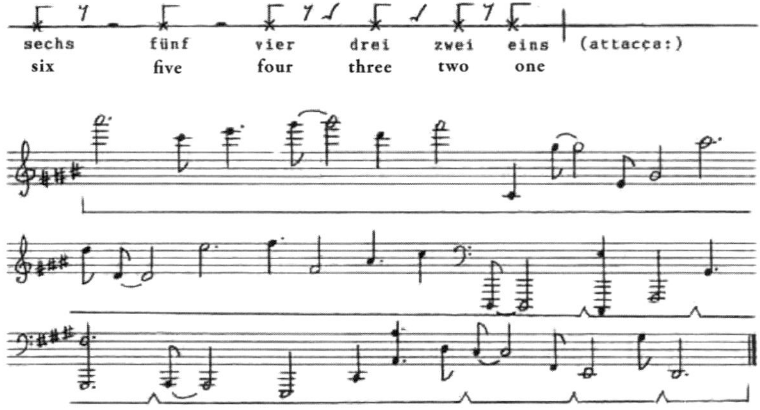

note

the numbers 1-6 spoken as an introduction also indicate their durations (1 = one second, 6 = six seconds). with the sensualization of the abstract numbers into concrete piano tones, these durations also apply to the six tones of the whole-tone scale. their sequence – first within the three-note, then within the two-note and the one-note, and finally the minor, major, and contra-octave – was determined aleatorically. in this way the notes gain increasing weight, materiality, and rhythmic differentiation both in terms of expansion and their downward trend.

melodical strokes 1

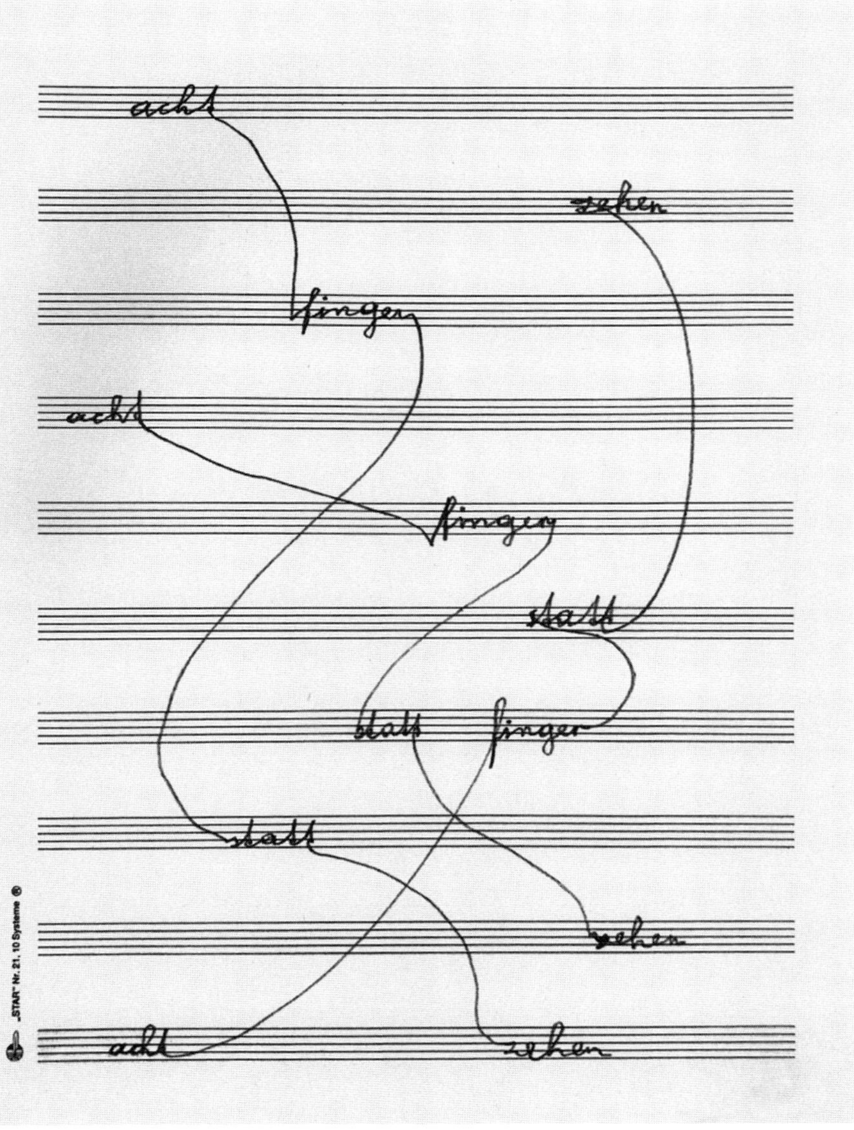

[acht = eight / fingern = fingers / zehen = toes / statt = instead of]

melodical strokes 2

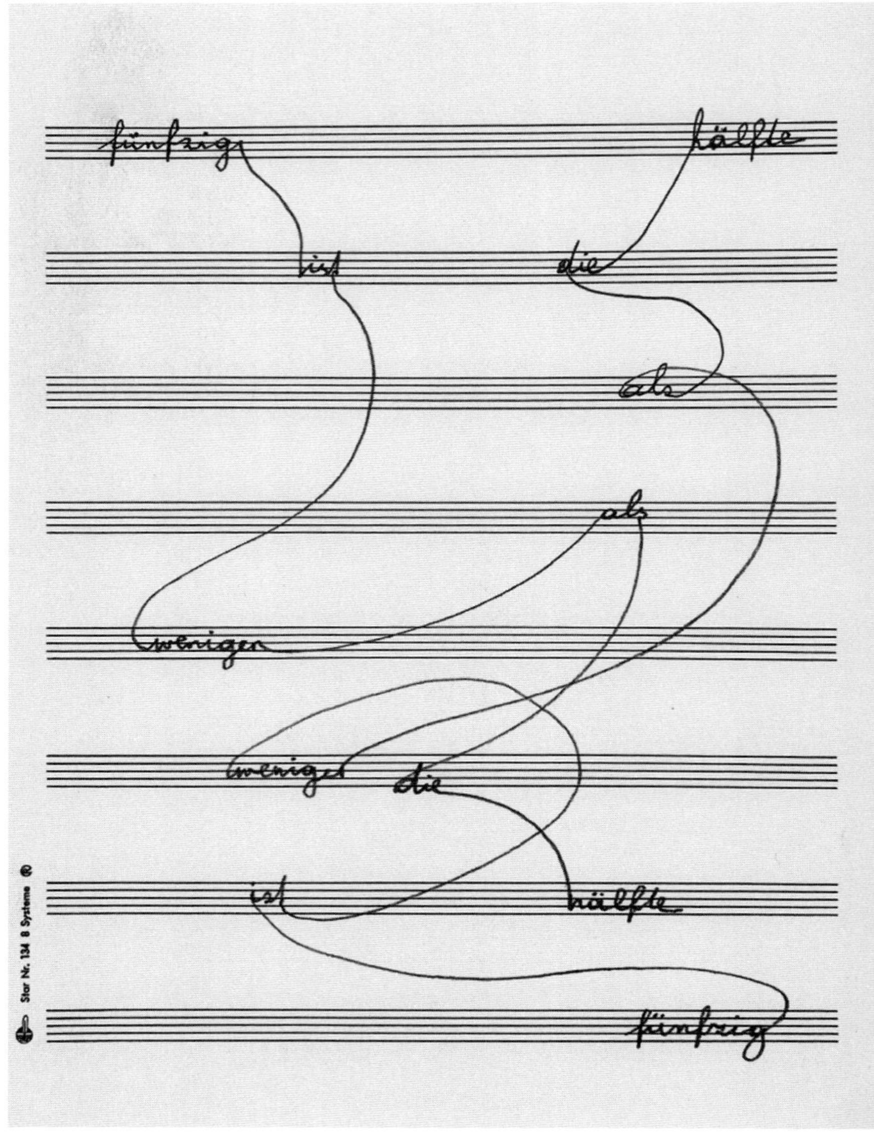

[fünfzig = fifty / hälfte = half / weniger = less (than) / als = than]

m1

[m + eins = mine]

1t

[eins + t = once]

so

one
and one
doubtful
desired

admired
thousands
swellions
shrillions

so
make
yours and mine
one

on monday
at one
on tuesday
at one thirty
on wednesday
and thursday
at three
or four
on friday
at five
on saturday
six
seven
on sunday
between eleven
and twelve
on monday
from eight
tuesday
till ten
on wednesday
around nine
on thursday
friday
and saturday
at one already
on sunday
and monday
tuesday
and wednesday
at two
three
four

six
nine
hundred
thousand
million
you me
you me
you me

all

i am
alone
in twos
in threes
in fives
in tens
in hundreds
amid the crowded square
in the city
in the countryside
on earth
in the whole wide world

sonnet

first stanza first line
first stanza second line
first stanza third line
first stanza fourth line

second stanza first line
second stanza second line
second stanza third line
second stanza fourth line

third stanza first line
third stanza second line
third stanza third line

fourth stanza first line
fourth stanza second line
fourth stanza third line

imperfect counting poem

one
two
three
four
five
six
seven
eight
nine
toes

one's missing

which of the elves?

one,
two,
three,
four,
five
six,
seven,
eight?
nein –
already the tenth
of the elves!

in the waiting room

a forest piece

two
four
six
eight
nine
seven
five
three
one
two
three
four
five
six
seven
eight
nine
ten
eleven elves
waiting on the twelfth

a long wait
real long

the twelve apostles

the first
    was ready to burst
the second
    was with no weapon
the third
    was of the herd
the fourth
    was off for the north
the fifth
    was all full of pith
the sixth
    was all full of piss
the seventh
    was never a peasant
the eighth
    was of little faith
the ninth
    was bloated with wine
the tenth
    was totally spent
the eleventh
    was all but present
the twelfth
    was up the ladder
    when he realized, shit, my bladder

tabula rasa

two minus three
fifteen minus sixteen
seven-hundred-ninety minus seven-hundred-ninety-one
eight-thousand-five-hundred-twenty-one minus eight-thousand-five-hundred-twenty-two
four-million-seven-thousand-six-hundred minus four-million-seven-thousand-six-hundred-one
nine-billion-five-million-four-thousand-eight-hundred-thirty minus nine-billion-five-million-four-thousand-eight-hundred-thirty-one

after nine-billion-and-nine-thousand-two-million-one-thousand-seven-hundred-and-fifty-eight pieces of furniture and utensils disappeared without a trace, seven surplus zeros fizzled out like nothing into an inexistent space

32 birds
32 birds

1 round

32 birds
32 birds

1 round
32 birds

32 birds
1 round

1 round
32 birds
32 birds
32 birds

(who sees the
32 birds)
1 round
1 round

(when were they killed the
32 birds)
32 birds
32 birds

9 rounds
9 rounds
9 rounds

32 birds
32 birds
32 birds

41

1 and 1 is 1 and 1
2 is 2
still
1 and 1 is 1 and 1
2 is not 1 and 1
but
2 is 2
and
1 and 1 is not 2
but
1 and 1
this is how
the birds' lives begin
and
how they end

sixty-nine pairs of lovers

69 69 69 69 69 69 69 69 69 69

69 69 69 69 69 69 69 69 69 69

69 69 69 69 69 69 69 69 69 69

69 69 69 69 69 69 69 69 69 69

69 69 69 69 69 69 69 69 69 69

69 69 69 69 69 69 69 69 69 69

69 69 69 69 69 69 69 69 69

hasty statistic

3 advantages
3 disadvantages
3 parts

6 parts

9 advantages
9 disadvantages
10 parts
(haste makes waste)

13 l
hasty hasty hasty
12 x daily
(before 12
after 12)

2 hatchets on a stump
makes
3 to hump
3 to hump
and one shaft
makes
4 daft

55 trials
(64 vials for the common good)

99 piles and dials
per (before) mile (after)

50 arrows hurry
yearly to
49 furries
(why not wait)

138 likes for smart swine (2 each)
(-12 lazy peeps per line)

blades + bumps

all (-all)

3 busty babes jump
9 to hump
all to no avail
(12 in every case
p.s. :
were one to race and call
before going on to ball a total of 6 x down the hall
(9 advantages give
12 disadvantages with one advantage per person)

only one column per hall
e.g. choose a column before every ball when
2 halls with 3 columns fall
(if anyone squints at the numbers after each call)

in short :
dash dash dash
9 x cash
count how many
hard-earned pennies
188 aims per person (therefore 1 half man per line)

bare stems
brumal steel
squish
948 jellyfish
in the field

(bottom line :)
no time!

mezzanine
1st floor
2nd floor
3rd floor
1st staircase
4th floor
ground floor
2nd staircase
courtyard
2nd staircase
elevator
door 22
cellar
5th floor
3rd staircase
4th staircase
door 8
9
wall
10

the resurrection of the flesh

for hermann nitsch

at eight
up goes the hair
at nine
the eyelids lift
at ten
the mouth opens
at eleven
up goes the left hand
at twelve
up goes the right
at one
up goes the head
at two
up go the arms
at three
the upper body straightens
at four
the body slips to its knees
at five
the leg stiffens
at six
the whole man stands tall
at seven
up goes his schlong, trills a moist little song —
then everything falls to ash
amen

i mean all of you

while the first argue with the second and third
about all they've incorrectly heard
the fourth are busy staring at the fifth
who are wrinkling their noses at all they've missed

if the if were not

ten biddies
from six different cities
at loggerheads
to see
if eleven beds
are really
a pity
and if the neat
somewhat effete
eleventh geezer
with tweezers
is witty
and if the gritty
ditty being played
throughout eleven cities
sounds pretty
sounds pretty.

through and through

after a hundred men
from the hundredth to the thousandth had come
from a thousand meters up
a jack-of-all-trades
tossed out a thousand times a thousand kisses
to a thousandth of them
causing them to die a thousand deaths.
"mon deux," he said, before
adding, as the last one alive :
"through and through!"

definitive

nullifying itself
with pleasure
the naught naughts
all at leisure

awaiting nil
it nullifies time
and nothings space
erasing life's thrill

with zero zips
despite zero debts
the haughty naught naughts
with all it's got : "diddly squat!"

only

A relatively quiet week
on Austria's roads
Only eight people
lost their lives

due to accidents.
Whereas eighteen died
during the same week
the previous year.

19.04.1997

daily routine

seven hours of waiting
in the eighth a shock
in the ninth a wait
in the tenth collected stuff
in the eleventh scattered again
in the twelfth fell asleep

in the first hour awoke
in the second amazed
in the third called out
in the fourth a wait
in the fifth once and back again
in the sixth took a seat

memories

two-hundred times over
sixteen-billion times over
ten times over
four-hundred-seventy-eight-thousand-nine-hundred-and-ten times over
twenty-seven-trillion-three-hundred-and-twelve times over
not a single time over
two times over
nine-thousand-and-five times over
seven-hundred-eighty-thousand-four-hundred-and-twenty times over
nineteen times over
thirty-two-trillion times over
nine-hundred-thirty-five-thousand-and-a-half times over
zero-point-six times over
zero-point-five times over
eight-hundred-forty-three times over
seventy-thousand-two-hundred-ninety-one times over
forty-five-thousand-eight-hundred-thirty-two-million times over
seventeen-billion-two-hundred-and-eleven-million-one-thousand-and-
two times over
thirteen times over
seventeen times over
sixty-eight times over
four-hundred-twenty-seven times over
one time
twenty-four times over

birthday

i was never one hour old
or ever one year
i never turned 12
or ever turned 20
i was never 42
or 63 either
i was never younger or older
than NOW

a drama in five acts

curtain rises.
on the darkened stage five people standing next to one another. each of them holding a burning candle in their hand.
after a little while, the second person (from the left) blows the first person's candle out. exit first person.
now the third person blows the second person's candle out. exit second person.
the fourth person blows the third person's candle out. exit third person.
the fifth person blows the fourth person's candle out. exit fourth person.
the fifth person looks around for a little while, at a loss. then blows out own candle. total darkness.
curtain falls.

variation on a familiar theme

of ten one dropped
of nine only eight remained
of eight only seven
of seven only six
of six only five
of five only four
of the four, yep, you guessed it, only three
and these too decreased further still
until suddenly the remaining two became
a pair
and each half of the pair was afraid
of ultimately being left alone
for it seemed inevitable
but that wouldn't take too long either

nine!

one
two
three
four
five
six
seven
suspicion

one
two
three
four
five
six
seven
sparked

one
two
three
four
five
six
seven
teased

one
two
three

four
five
six
seven
bequeathed

one
two
three
four
five
six
seven
the freight

one
two
three
four
five
six
seven
by the gate

one
two
three
four
five
six
seven
all night

one
two
three
four
five
six
seven
eyes white

an austrian counting poem

(after a statement from the general secretary of the austrian people's party)

not one,
not two,
not three,
not four,
not even five,
only when, "Waldheim strangled six Jews with his own hands is there a problem."

history

a note on recitation

the pause between the first and second line is very long (long enough to keep the listeners tense), whereas the span between the second and third line is noticeably shorter. from then on, the pauses shorten continuously until the NOW that follows the "just." at the same time, starting with the eighth line, the dynamics increase rapidly from a normal tone to an exalted cry. following NOW, the duration of the pauses as well as the volume begin to ebb.

one billion years ago
one million years ago
one thousand years ago
one hundred years ago
before my birth
ten years ago
one year ago
one month ago
one week ago
yesterday
one hour ago
just
NOW
soon
in one hour
tomorrow
in one week
in one month
in one year
in ten years

after my death
in one hundred years
in one thousand years
in one million years
in one billion years

line for line

the first of the lines doesn't think it's fine,
so encourages the second to really shine.
the third says : reader, go ahead and take your time,
take your time and linger on the fourth and very best line.

pigeon coo

at one o'clock
without further ado
the pigeon gawks
and says "coo, coo."
at two o'clock,
without further ado
the pigeon gawks
and says "coo, coo."
at three o'clock,
without further ado
the pigeon gawks
and says "coo, coo."
if up to twelve she's just playing around,
come two she really goes to town.

viennese dialect poem 1

amoe ka zweidds moe
zwamoe ka dridds moe
dreimoe ka viadds moe
viamoe ka fümbbfds moe
fümfmoe seggsmoe sibm ochd neinmoe zenmoe öfmoe des is
schee

once not two times
two times not three
three times not four
four times not five
five times six times seven eight nine times ten times eleven times
how fine

viennese dialect poem 2

a halsal 1 keddn a freid
1 kedden a halsal a freid
a freid 1 keddn a halsal
1 keddn a freid a halsal
a halsal a freid 1 keddn
a freid a halsal 1 kedden

a little neck 1 necklace a joy
1 necklace a little neck a joy
a joy 1 necklace a little neck
1 necklace a joy a little neck
a little neck a joy 1 necklace
a joy a little neck 1 necklace

birthday party

a young australian girl posted an invitation to her sixteenth birthday party on facebook. she gave her address and told her classmates to come and bring friends. at first she was afraid that no one would come.
but but
within within within
only only only only
twenty-four twenty-four twenty-four twenty-four twenty-four
(6x) hours hours hours hours hours hours
(7x) twenty-thousand twenty-thousand twenty-thousand twenty-thousand twenty-thousand twenty-thousand twenty-thousand
(8x) facebook-users facebook-users facebook-users facebook-users facebook-users facebook-users facebook-users facebook-users
(9x) had had had had had had had had had
(10) rsvped rsvped rsvped rsvped rsvped rsvped rsvped rsvped rsvped rsvped
(11) as as as as as as as as as as as
(12) guests guests guests guests guests guests guests guests guests guests guests guests
(13) the the the the the the the the the the the the the
(14) next next next next next next next next next next next next next next
(15) day day day day day day day day day day day day day day day
(16) there there there there there there there there there there there there there there there there
(17) were were were were were were were were were were were were were were were were were
(18) now now now now now now now now now now now now now now now now now now
(19) almost almost almost almost almost almost almost almost almost almost almost almost almost almost almost almost almost almost almost

(20) two-hundred-thousand

sense of time

a week ago i was still a child
five days ago i was an adult
four days ago was the time of the "vienna group"
three days ago i was living in berlin
for two days now i've been in cologne
everything since the turn of the millennium happened yesterday
since early this morning i haven't aged at all

an unpleasant counting poem

at half past one
it was already three
at half past seven
it was still night
at five to four
there was someone here
it was shortly after ten
when they disappeared

a christian arithmetic lesson

a polish book on mathematics
came under criticism for its anti-turkish take.

in the elementary school textbook children were asked
to calculate how to ensure that a ship, were it to sink, sailed
by turks and christians would only have christians left.

according to the catholic weekly *tygodnik powszechny*
the book's publisher and co-author denied
any kind of racist motives. they replied
it was a simple case of mathematics.

a bruckner anecdote

count letters
count letters
count letters
count letters
count letters
count letters

---

six

---

count candles
count candles
count candles
count candles
count candles
count candles
count candles
count candles
count candles
count candles

---

ten

---

count stairs
count stairs
count stairs
count stairs
count stairs
count stairs
count stairs
count stairs
count stairs
count stairs
count stairs

---

eleven

---

count stars
stars . . .

mortal intercourse

the first observes the distant sixth,
who leaned against the tenth,
who yearns for the eleventh, beside the tenth.
who reveres the first.

the first tests the sixth :
who calls the tenth "ten."
the tenth counts to eleven.
while the eleventh treasures the first.

the first appraises the sixth,
who goes without the tenth,
who recognizes the eleventh.
the eleventh takes care of the first.

the first discusses the sixth,
who desires the tenth.
the tenth opts for the eleventh,
who nourishes the first.

the first teaches the sixth,
who confuses the tenth with another.
the tenth defuses the eleventh,
who illumines the first.

the first converts the sixth,
who is missing the tenth.
the tenth tames the eleventh,
who fakes the first.

the first arranges the sixth,
who blinds the tenth.
the tenth washes the eleventh,
who sticks to the first.

the first twists the sixth,
who hounds the tenth.
the tenth straightens out the eleventh,
who documents the first.

the first weakens the sixth,
who disfigures the tenth.
the tenth lifts the eleventh,
who annoys the first.

the first blackmails the sixth,
who conceals the tenth.
the tenth carries the eleventh,
who scares off the first.

the first hits the sixth,
who expands the tenth.
the tenth hassles the eleventh,
who excites the first.

the first dominates the sixth,
who propagates the tenth.
the tenth cramps the eleventh,
who covers the first.

the first uses the sixth,
who strengthens the tenth.
the tenth waters the eleventh,
who empties the first.

the first blesses the sixth,
who hurts the tenth.
the tenth licks the eleventh,
who replaces the burning first.

the sixth gives the tenth
away to the eleventh, who falls asleep next to the deeply desired tenth.
thinking of the first, the tenth, the eleventh, the sixth tells
the just recently discovered and far away sixteenth he
should have
observed,
yearned,
revered,
tested,
counted,
treasured
appraised,
gone without,
taken care of,
discussed,
desired,
chosen,
nourished,
taught,
confused,
defused,
illumined,
converted,
missed,
tamed,
faked,
arranged,
blinded,

stuck,
twisted,
hounded,
straightened,
documented,
weakened,
disfigured,
annoyed,
blackmailed,
concealed,
scared off,
expanded,
hassled,
excited,
dominated,
propagated,
cramped,
covered,
used,
strengthened,
watered,
emptied,
blessed,
hurt,
licked,
replaced,
given away.
furthermore:
due to the end of the first, the tenth, the eleventh, the last, he, the sixth, now brings himself to an end.

climate change

a joke that gets out of hand

someone who's died of the heat meets someone who's died of the cold. the former's got a question but doesn't have any air. the latter might respond were it not for his mouth frozen shut.
two others who've died of the heat meet two others who've died of the cold. both of the former have questions, but don't have any air. both of the latter might respond were it not for their mouths frozen shut.
three others who've died of the heat meet three more who've died of the cold. they too have questions, but don't have any air. the latter might respond were it not for their mouths frozen shut.
ten others who've died of the heat meet ten who've died of the cold. the former have questions, but don't have any air. all of the latter might respond were it not for their mouths frozen shut.
a hundred others who've died of the heat meet a hundred who've died of the cold. the former have questions, but don't have any air. all of the latter might respond were it not for their mouths frozen shut.
a thousand others who've died of the heat meet a thousand who've died of the cold. the former have questions, but don't have any air. all of the latter might respond were it not for their mouths frozen shut.
ten-thousand others who've died of the heat meet ten-thousand who've died of the cold. the former have questions, but don't have any air. all of the latter might respond were it not for their mouths frozen shut.
a hundred thousand others who've died of the heat meet a hundred thousand who've died of the cold. the former have questions, but don't have any air. all of the latter might respond were it not for their mouths frozen shut.
a million others who've died of the heat meet a million who've died of the cold. the former have questions, but don't have any air. all of the latter might respond were it not for their mouths frozen shut.
and so on, more and more and more and more and more

the misfortune of being lucky

operetta for one voice

act 1 slow foxtrot

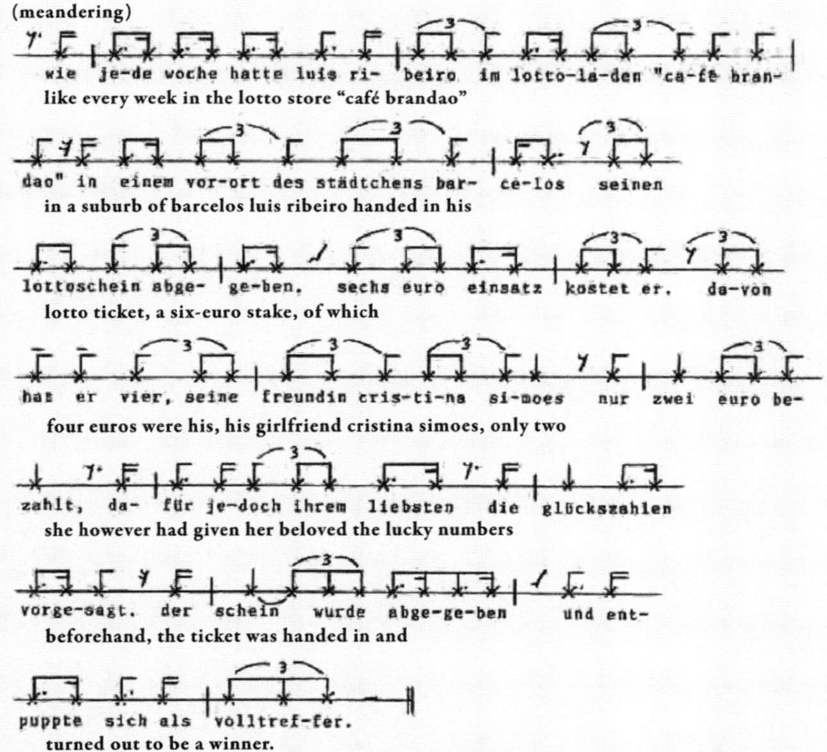

act 2 waltz and gallop

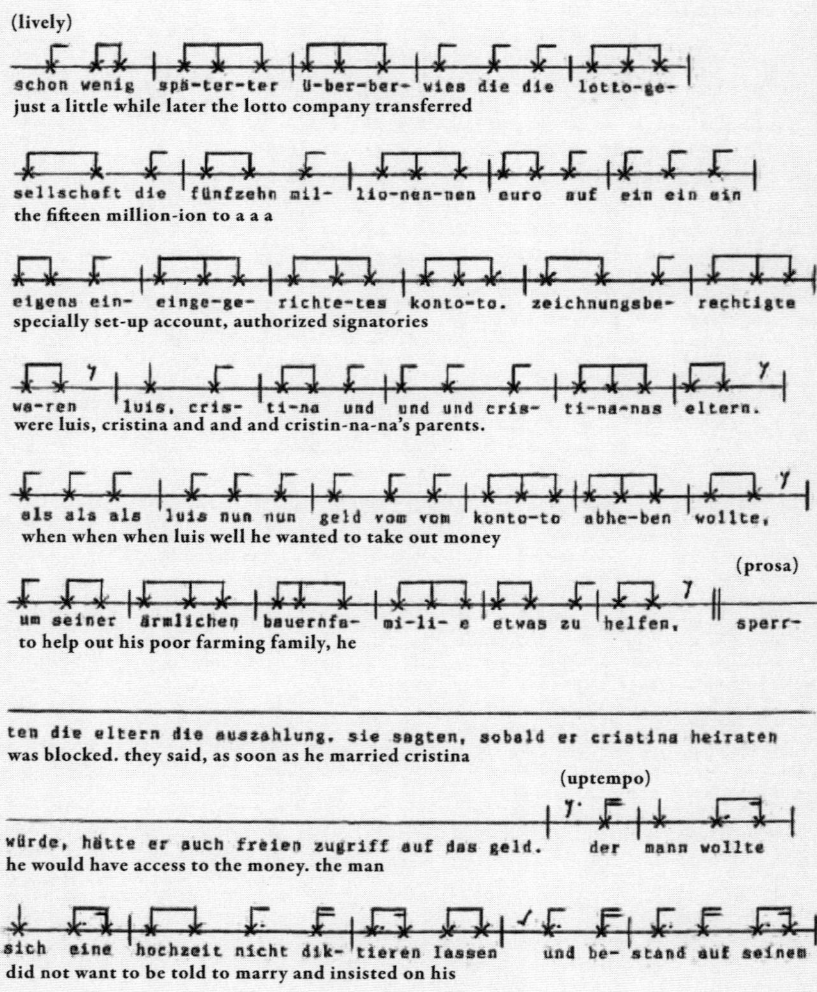

anteil: sieben-ein- halb millio-nen euro. der streit be-gann, es
share: seventeen-and-a-half million euros. the fight began, and

kam zu einem pro- zess. der vorschlag, die summe in zwei gleiche
ended up in court. the proposal of sharing the sum in two

hälften aufzu- teilen, wurde von der par- tei cris-ti-nas
equal halves was rejected by cristina's side

abge-lehnt und das geld auf richter- lichen beschluss eingefro-ren.
and the money, by order of the court, was frozen.

das paar war restlos zer- stritten.
the couple completely at odds.

act 3 funeral march and march

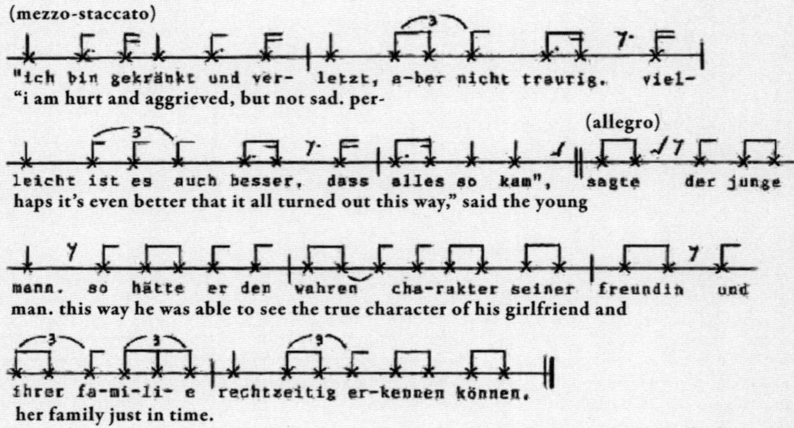

auction of a cracker from the "titanic"

spoken duet for one female and one male voice

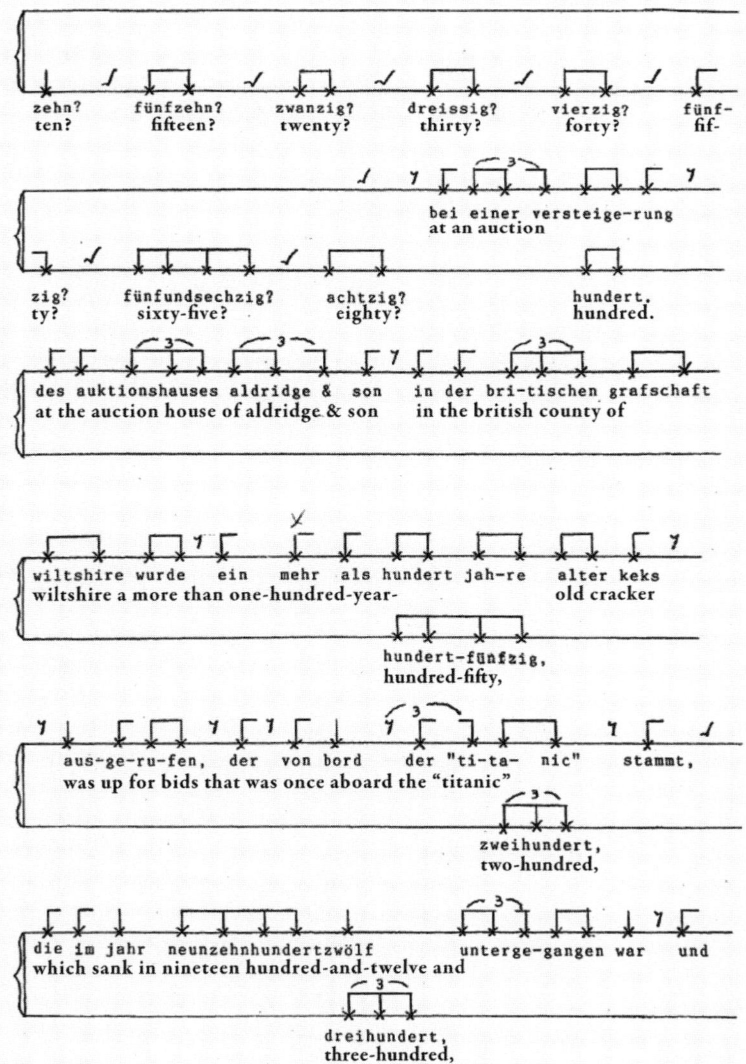

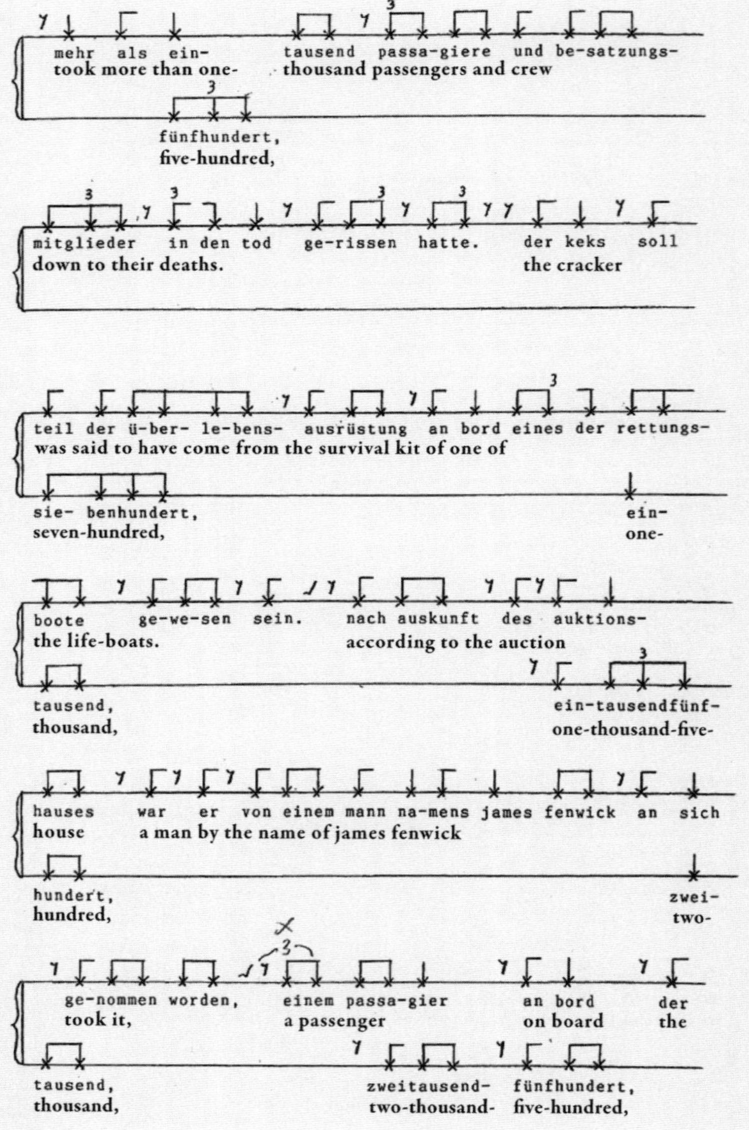
mehr als ein- tausend passa-giere und be-satzungs-
took more than one- thousand passengers and crew
fünfhundert,
five-hundred,
mitglieder in den tod ge-rissen hatte. der keks soll
down to their deaths. the cracker
teil der ü-ber- le-bens- ausrüstung an bord eines der rettungs-
was said to have come from the survival kit of one of
sie- benhundert,
seven-hundred,
ein-
one-
boote ge-we-sen sein. nach auskunft des auktions-
the life-boats. according to the auction
tausend,
thousand,
ein-tausendfünf-
one-thousand-five-
hauses war er von einem mann na-mens james fenwick an sich
house a man by the name of james fenwick
hundert,
hundred,
zwei-
two-
ge-nommen worden, einem passa-gier an bord der
took it, a passenger on board the
tausend,
thousand,
zweitausend- fünfhundert,
two-thousand- five-hundred,

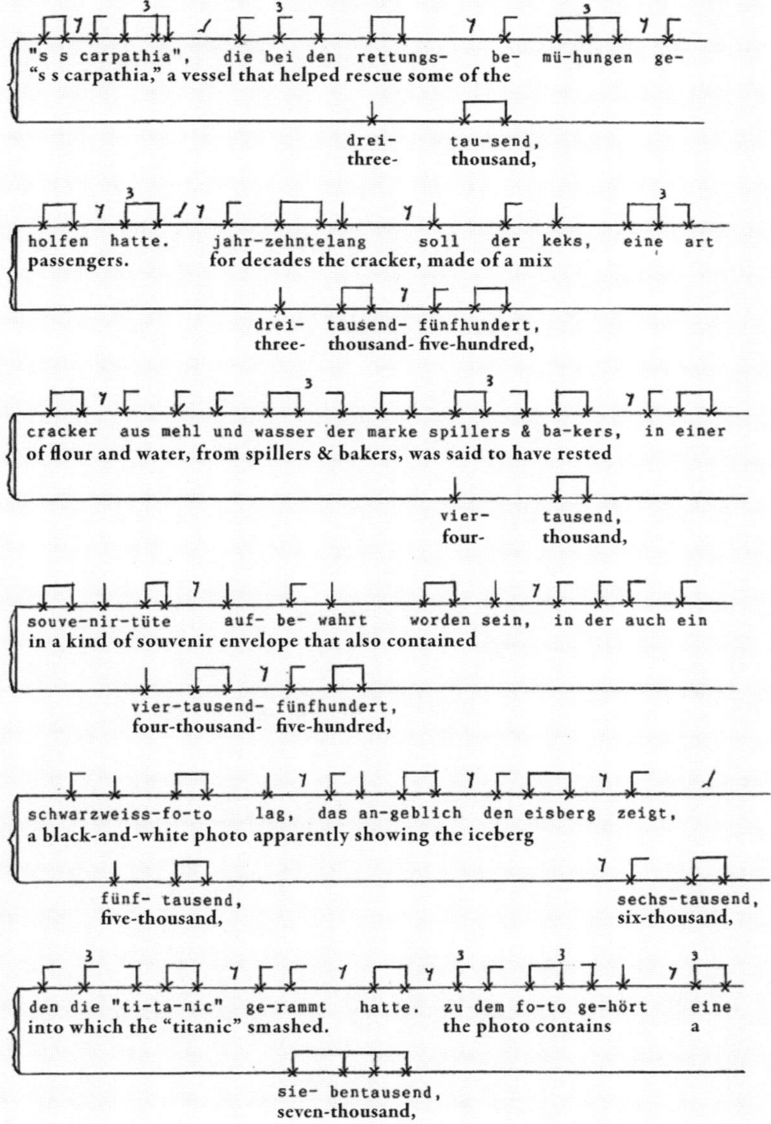
"s s carpathia", die bei den rettungs- be- mü-hungen ge-
"s s carpathia," a vessel that helped rescue some of the
drei- tau-send,
three- thousand,
holfen hatte. jahr-zehntelang soll der keks, eine art
passengers. for decades the cracker, made of a mix
drei- tausend- fünfhundert,
three- thousand- five-hundred,
cracker aus mehl und wasser der marke spillers & ba-kers, in einer
of flour and water, from spillers & bakers, was said to have rested
vier- tausend,
four- thousand,
souve-nir-tüte auf- be- wahrt worden sein, in der auch ein
in a kind of souvenir envelope that also contained
vier-tausend- fünfhundert,
four-thousand- five-hundred,
schwarzweiss-fo-to lag, das an-geblich den eisberg zeigt,
a black-and-white photo apparently showing the iceberg
fünf- tausend,
five-thousand,
sechs-tausend,
six-thousand,
den die "ti-ta-nic" ge-rammt hatte. zu dem fo-to ge-hört eine
into which the "titanic" smashed. the photo contains a
sie- bentausend,
seven-thousand,

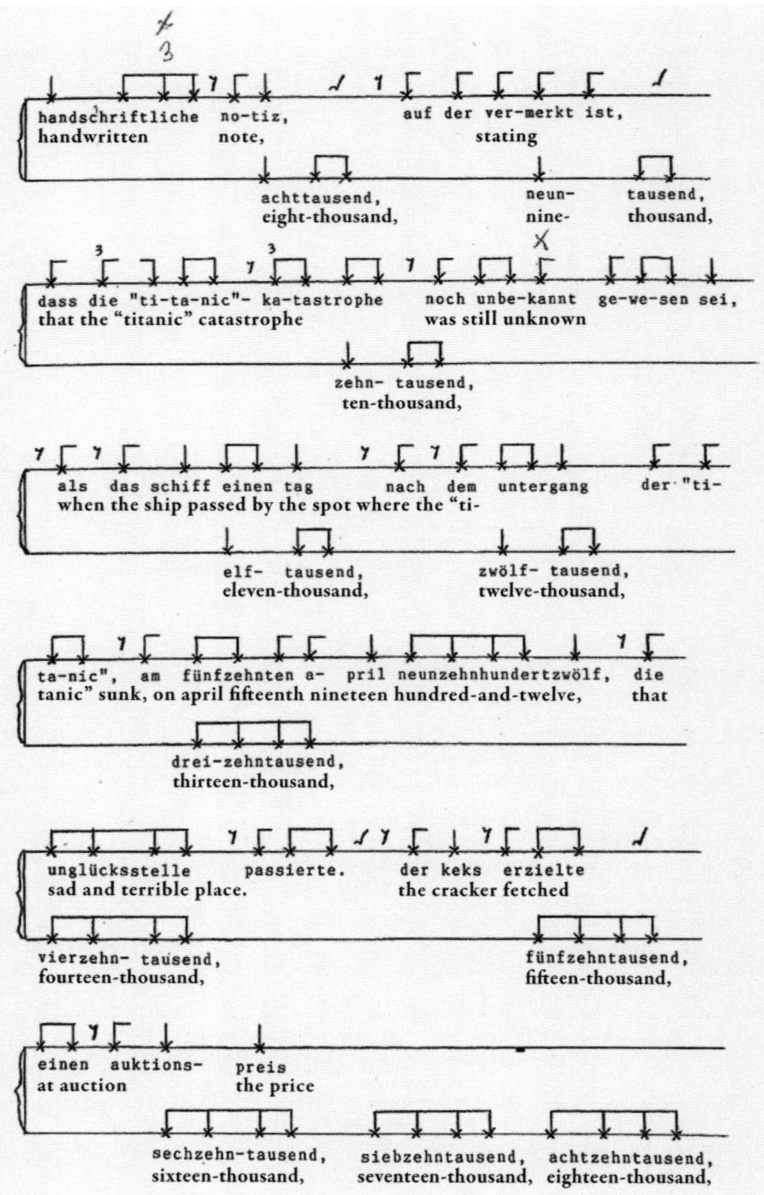
handschriftliche no-tiz, auf der ver-merkt ist,
handwritten note, stating
achttausend, neun- tausend,
eight-thousand, nine- thousand,
dass die "ti-ta-nic"- ka-tastrophe noch unbe-kannt ge-we-sen sei,
that the “titanic” catastrophe was still unknown
zehn- tausend,
ten-thousand,
als das schiff einen tag nach dem untergang der "ti-
when the ship passed by the spot where the “ti-
elf- tausend, zwölf- tausend,
eleven-thousand, twelve-thousand,
ta-nic", am fünfzehnten a- pril neunzehnhundertzwölf, die
tanic” sunk, on april fifteenth nineteen hundred-and-twelve, that
drei-zehntausend,
thirteen-thousand,
unglücksstelle passierte. der keks erzielte
sad and terrible place. the cracker fetched
vierzehn- tausend, fünfzehntausend,
fourteen-thousand, fifteen-thousand,
einen auktions- preis
at auction the price
sechzehn-tausend, siebzehntausend, achtzehntausend,
sixteen-thousand, seventeen-thousand, eighteen-thousand,

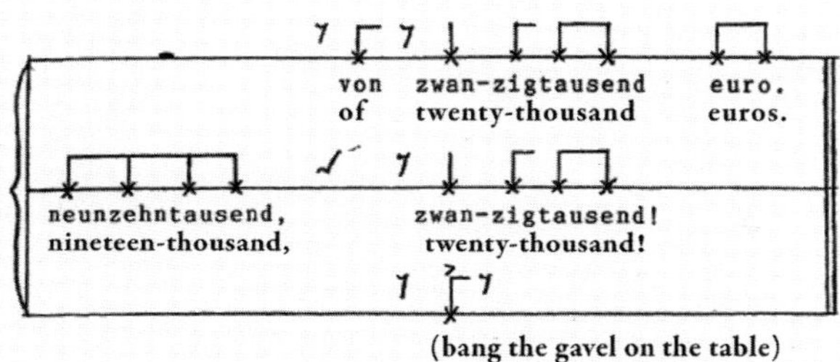
von zwan-zigtausend euro.
of twenty-thousand euros.
neunzehntausend, zwan-zigtausend!
nineteen-thousand, twenty-thousand!
(bang the gavel on the table)

setting sun and rising moon

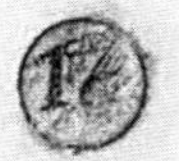

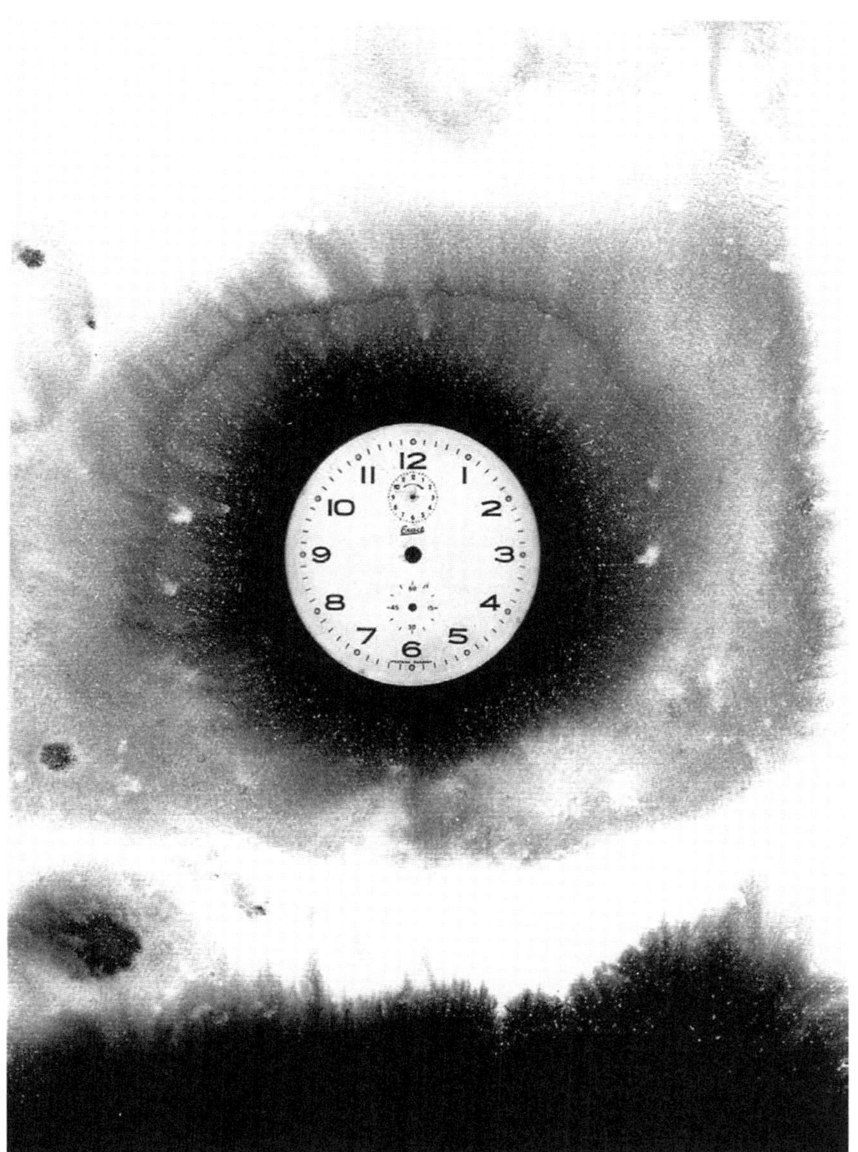
Exact

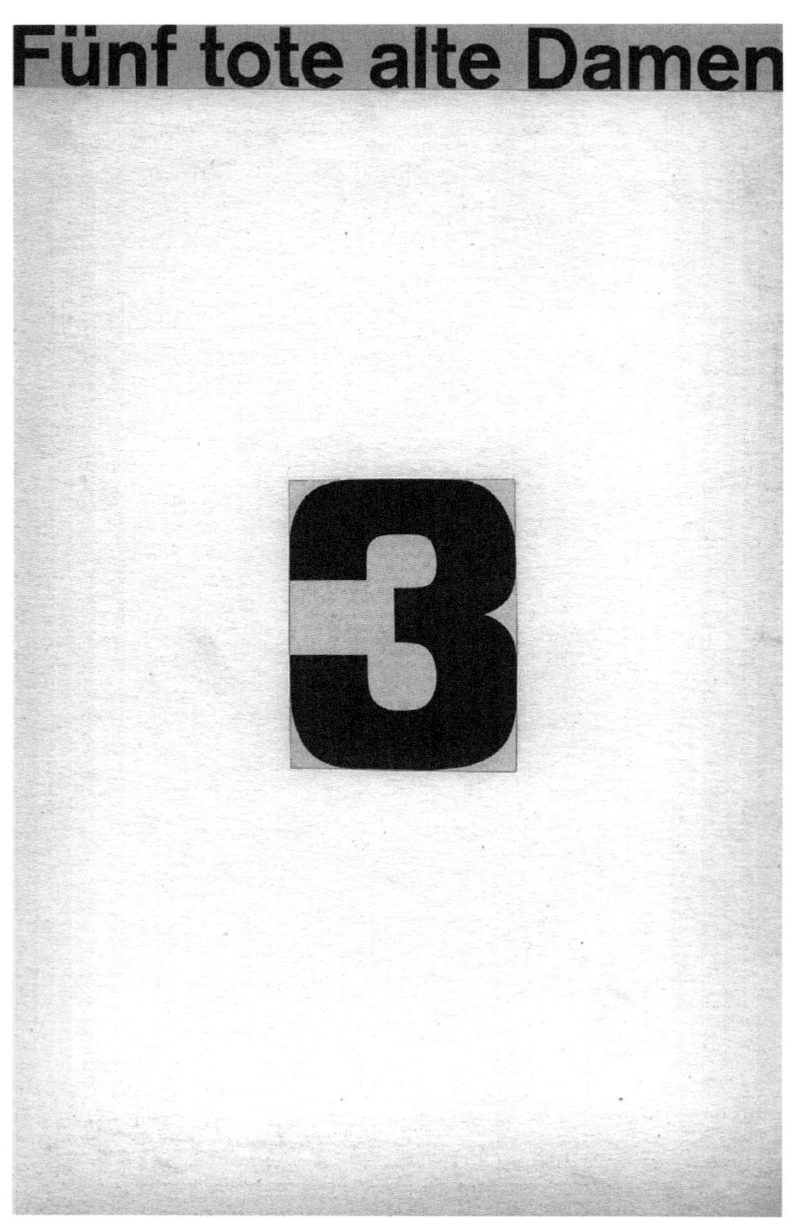

[five dead old women]

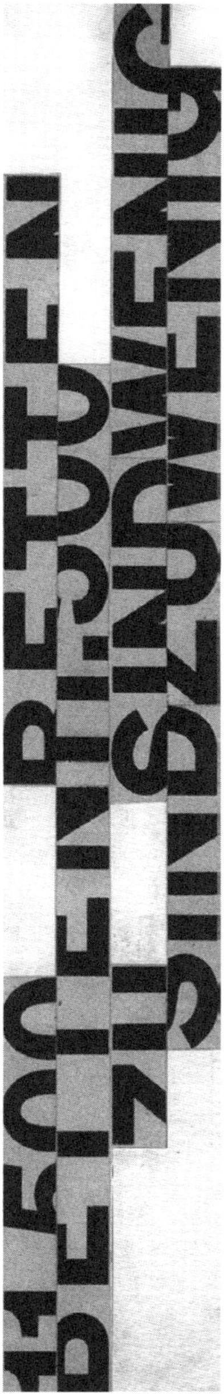

orthography

hunder17UND:·:zig

[one-hundred-fifty-seven]

Eintrittskarte
58
Nur mit Kontroll-Kupon gültig.
Auf Verlangen vorweisen.
77
„OMEGA" WIEN

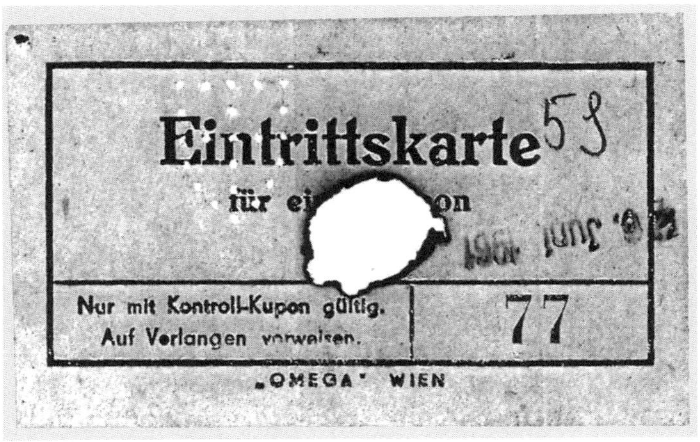

[ticket]

[n/one]

JUNI

1936 | 30 Tage | 1936

Juni						
S	M	D	M	D	F	S
—	1	2	3	4	5	6
7	8	9	10	11	12	13
14	15	16	17	18	19	20
21	22	23	24	25	26	27
28	29	30	—	—	—	—
—	—	—	—	—	—	—

2

Juli						
S	M	D	M	D	F	S
—	—	—	1	2	3	4
5	6	7	8	9	10	11
12	13	14	15	16	17	18
19	20	21	22	23	24	25
26	27	28	29	30	31	—
—	—	—	—	—	—	—

DIENSTAG

S.-A. 3.43 S.-U. 20.14
M.-A. 17.46 M.-U. 1.47

Strausberg?

Egons anrufen!

23. Woche Dienstag, 2. Juni 154—212

6

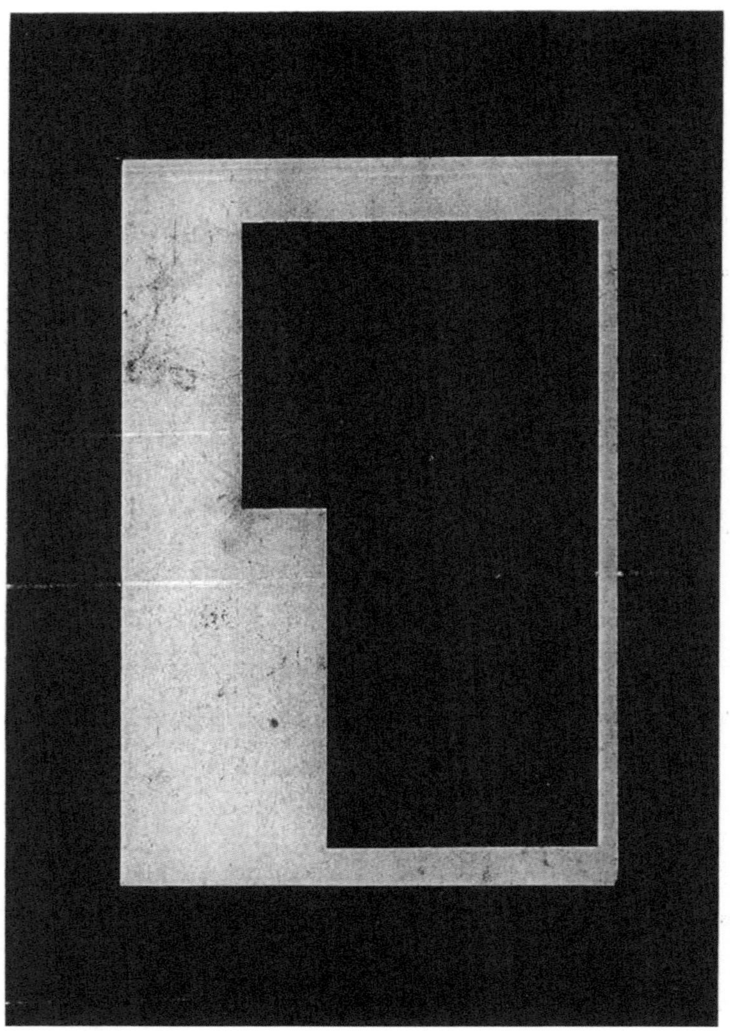

Größe: **110 x 140 cm**

693

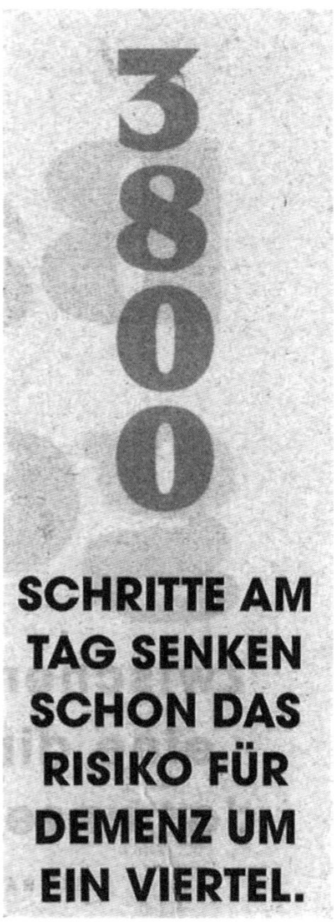

3800

SCHRITTE AM TAG SENKEN SCHON DAS RISIKO FÜR DEMENZ UM EIN VIERTEL.

[3800 steps per day reduces the risk of dementia by a fourth.]

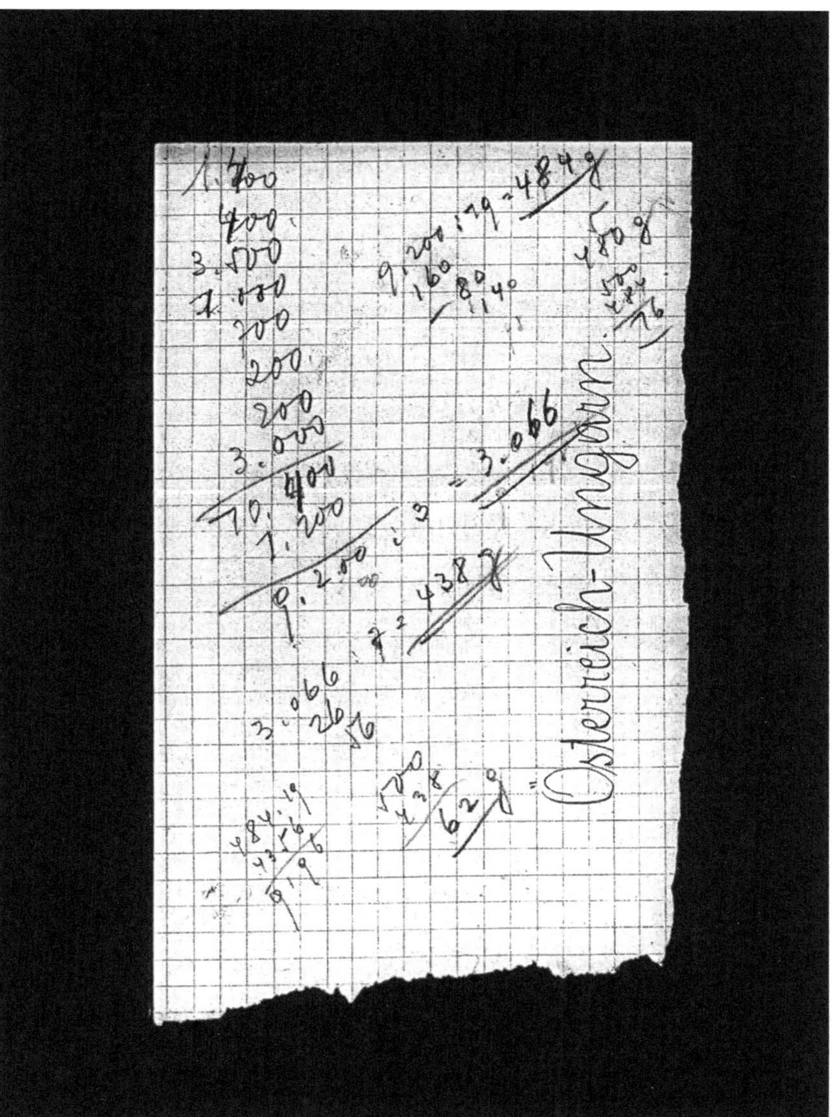
Österreich-Ungarn

[World's population increasing dramatically]

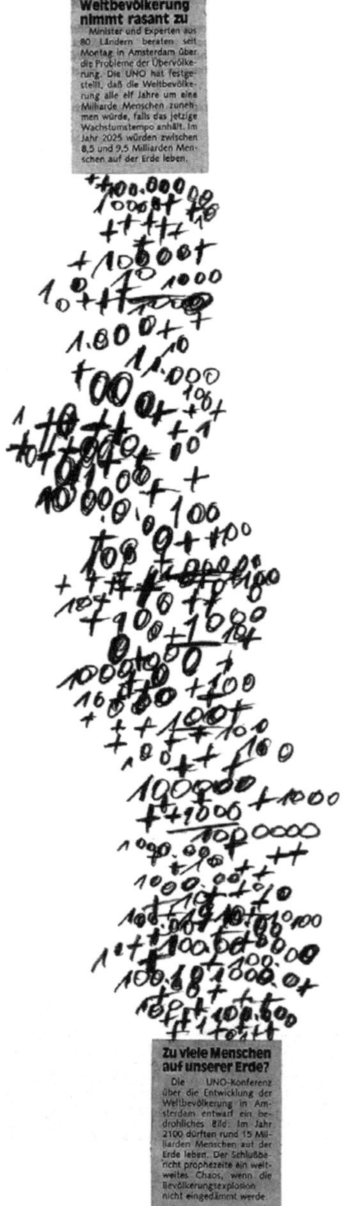

Weltbevölkerung nimmt rasant zu

Minister und Experten aus 80 Ländern beraten seit Montag in Amsterdam über die Probleme der Übervölkerung. Die UNO hat festgestellt, daß die Weltbevölkerung alle elf Jahre um eine Milliarde Menschen zunehmen würde, falls das jetzige Wachstumstempo anhält. Im Jahr 2025 würden zwischen 8,5 und 9,5 Milliarden Menschen auf der Erde leben.

Zu viele Menschen auf unserer Erde?

Die UNO-Konferenz über die Entwicklung der Weltbevölkerung in Amsterdam entwarf ein bedrohliches Bild: Im Jahr 2100 dürften rund 15 Milliarden Menschen auf der Erde leben. Der Schlußbericht prophezeite ein weltweites Chaos, wenn die Bevölkerungsexplosion nicht eingedämmt werde.

[Is our planet overpopulated?]

Alter	Männer	Frauen	Alter	Männer	Frauen	Alter	Männer	Frauen
18	59,42	64,69	45	33,54	38,28	72	12,07	14,57
19	58,42	63,71	46	32,63	37,34	73	11,44	13,80
20	57,49	62,73	47	31,72	36,40	74	10,82	13,05
21	56,53	61,73	48	30,83	35,46	75	10,23	12,31
22	55,56	60,75	49	29,94	34,53	76	9,66	11,59
23	54,59	59,76	50	29,06	33,60	77	9,11	10,89
24	53,63	58,78	51	28,19	32,68	78	8,58	10,21
25	52,66	57,79	52	27,33	31,76	79	8,07	9,56
26	51,69	56,80	53	26,48	30,85	80	7,56	8,92
27	50,73	55,82	54	25,64	29,95	81	7,08	8,32
28	49,76	54,83	55	24,80	29,04	82	6,62	7,74
29	48,79	53,84	56	23,98	28,15	83	6,19	7,19
30	47,82	52,86	57	23,16	27,26	84	5,78	6,67
31	46,85	51,87	58	22,34	26,37	85	5,39	6,17
32	45,88	50,89	59	21,54	25,49	86	5,04	5,73
33	44,92	49,91	60	20,75	24,61	87	4,70	5,30
34	43,95	48,93	61	19,97	23,74	88	4,38	4,89
35	42,99	47,95	62	19,19	22,88	89	4,04	4,49
36	42,03	46,97	63	18,43	22,02	90	3,73	4,13
37	41,07	45,99	64	17,68	21,17	91	3,45	3,81
38	40,11	45,02	65	16,93	20,31	92	3,23	3,52
39	39,15	44,04	66	16,20	19,46	93	3,03	3,29
40	38,20	43,08	67	15,48	18,62	94	2,84	3,07
41	37,26	42,11	68	14,76	17,79	95	2,66	2,87
42	36,32	41,15	69	14,07	16,96	96	2,49	2,70
43	35,38	40,19	70	13,38	16,15	97	2,34	2,52
44	34,46	39,23	71	12,71	15,35	98	2,20	2,36

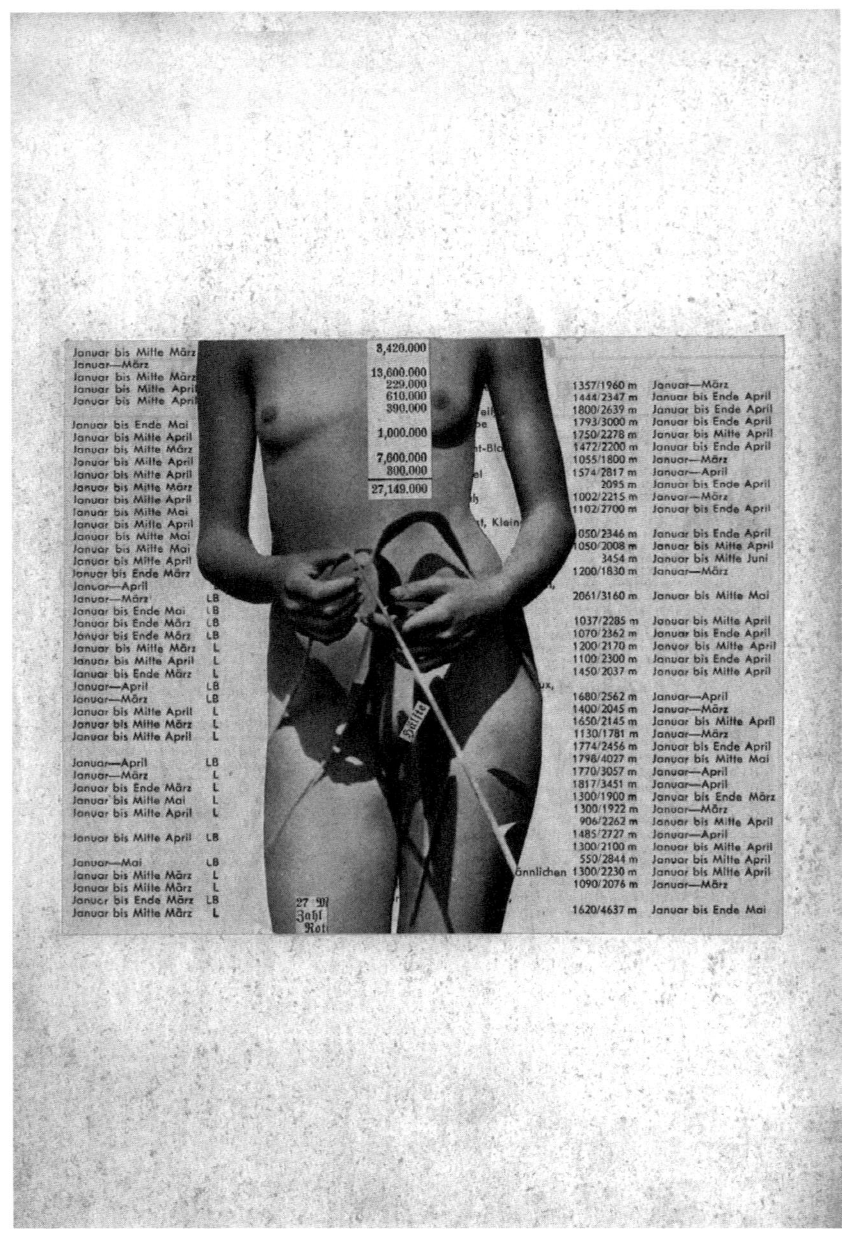
Januar bis Mitte März
Januar—März
Januar bis Mitte März
Januar bis Mitte April
Januar bis Mitte April
Januar bis Ende Mai
Januar bis Mitte April
Januar bis Mitte März
Januar bis Mitte April
Januar bis Mitte April
Januar bis Mitte März
Januar bis Mitte April
Januar bis Mitte Mai
Januar bis Mitte April
Januar bis Mitte Mai
Januar bis Mitte Mai
Januar bis Mitte April
Januar bis Ende März
Januar—April
Januar—März LB
Januar bis Ende Mai LB
Januar bis Ende März LB
Januar bis Ende März LB
Januar bis Mitte März L
Januar bis Mitte April L
Januar bis Ende März L
Januar—April LB
Januar—März LB
Januar bis Mitte April L
Januar bis Mitte März L
Januar bis Mitte April L
Januar—April LB
Januar—März L
Januar bis Ende März L
Januar bis Mitte Mai L
Januar bis Mitte April L
Januar bis Mitte April LB
Januar—Mai LB
Januar bis Mitte März L
Januar bis Mitte März L
Januar bis Ende März LB
Januar bis Mitte März L
8,420.000
13,600.000
229.000
610.000
390.000
1,000.000
7,600.000
800.000
27,149.000
Hälfte
1357/1960 m Januar—März
1444/2347 m Januar bis Ende April
1800/2639 m Januar bis Ende April
1793/3000 m Januar bis Ende April
1750/2278 m Januar bis Mitte April
1472/2200 m Januar bis Ende April
1055/1800 m Januar—März
1574/2817 m Januar—April
2095 m Januar bis Ende April
1002/2215 m Januar—März
1102/2700 m Januar bis Ende April
1050/2346 m Januar bis Ende April
1050/2008 m Januar bis Mitte April
3454 m Januar bis Mitte Juni
1200/1830 m Januar—März
2061/3160 m Januar bis Mitte Mai
1037/2285 m Januar bis Mitte April
1070/2362 m Januar bis Ende April
1200/2170 m Januar bis Mitte April
1100/2300 m Januar bis Ende April
1450/2037 m Januar bis Mitte April
1680/2562 m Januar—April
1400/2045 m Januar—März
1650/2145 m Januar bis Mitte April
1130/1781 m Januar—März
1774/2456 m Januar bis Ende April
1798/4027 m Januar bis Mitte Mai
1770/3057 m Januar—April
1817/3451 m Januar—April
1300/1900 m Januar bis Ende März
1300/1922 m Januar—März
906/2262 m Januar bis Mitte April
1485/2727 m Januar—April
1300/2100 m Januar bis Mitte April
550/2844 m Januar bis Mitte April
1300/2230 m Januar bis Mitte April
1090/2076 m Januar—März
1620/4637 m Januar bis Ende Mai

			8		1			
		4		3		2		
	9		7		4		1	
9		8				7		5
	6						9	
5		2				3		6
	2		1		6		5	
		5		9		8		
			2		8			

DOLLS			
SKIN			

SAILS			
HORSES			

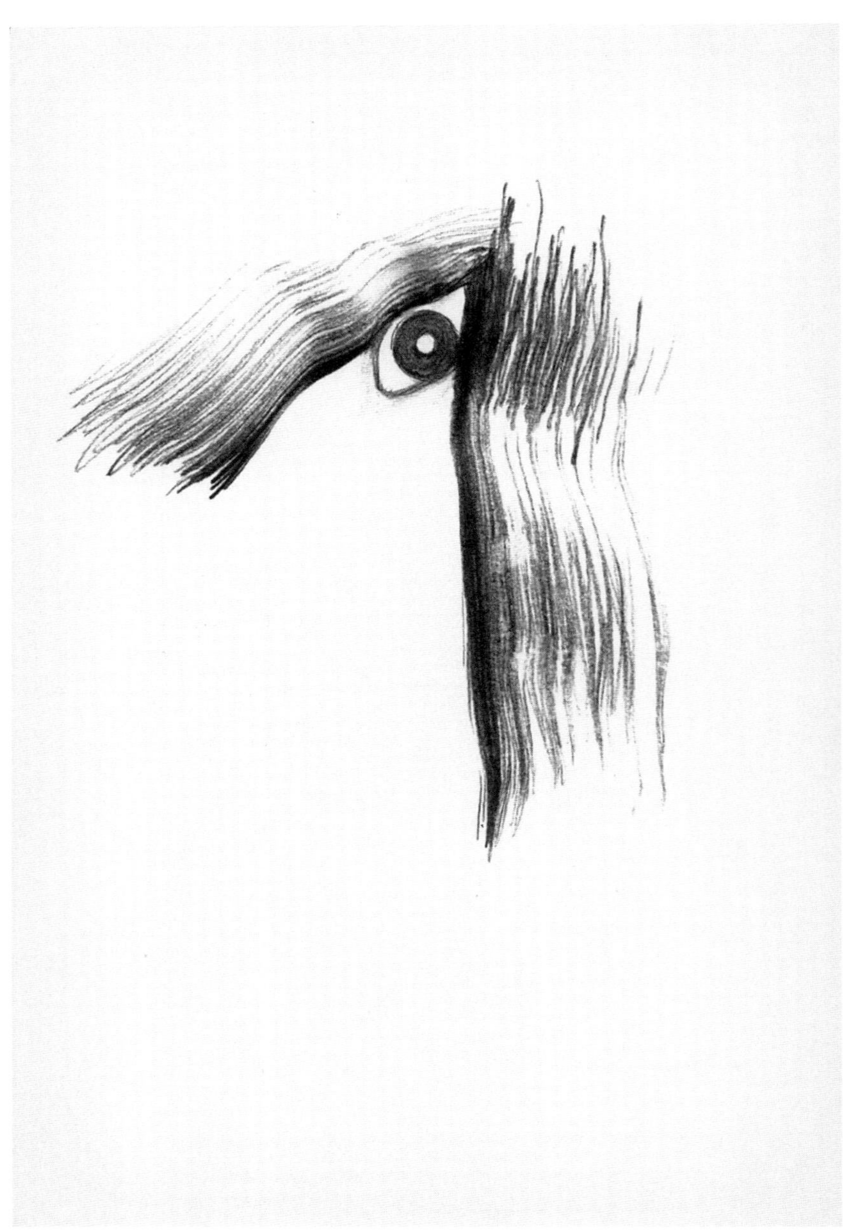

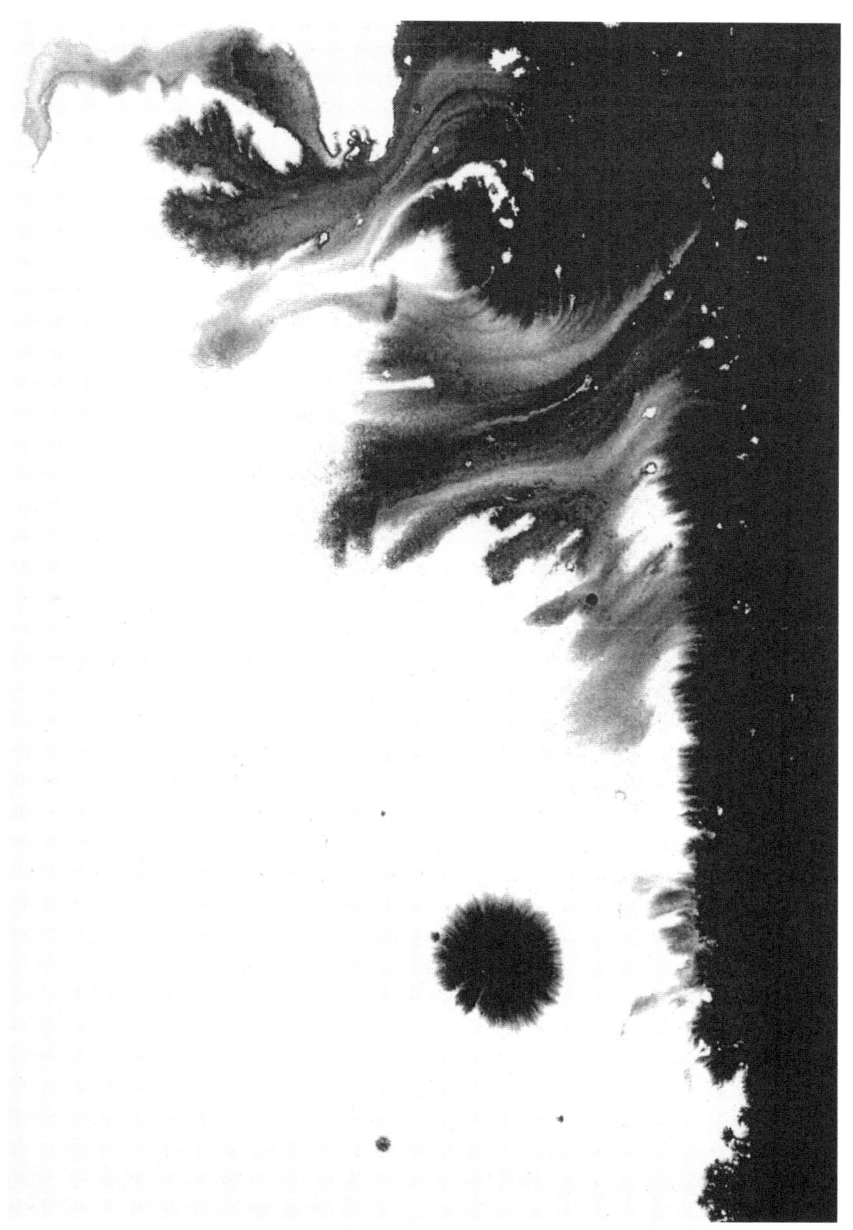

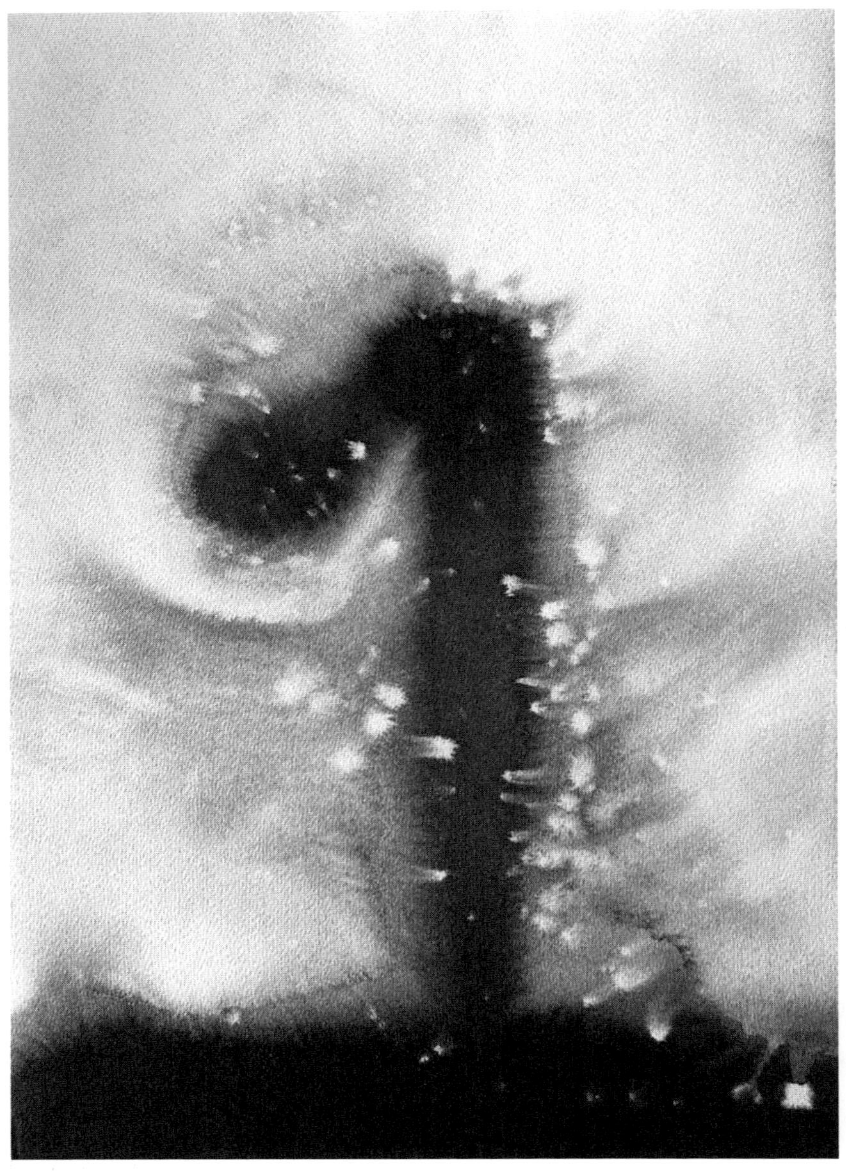

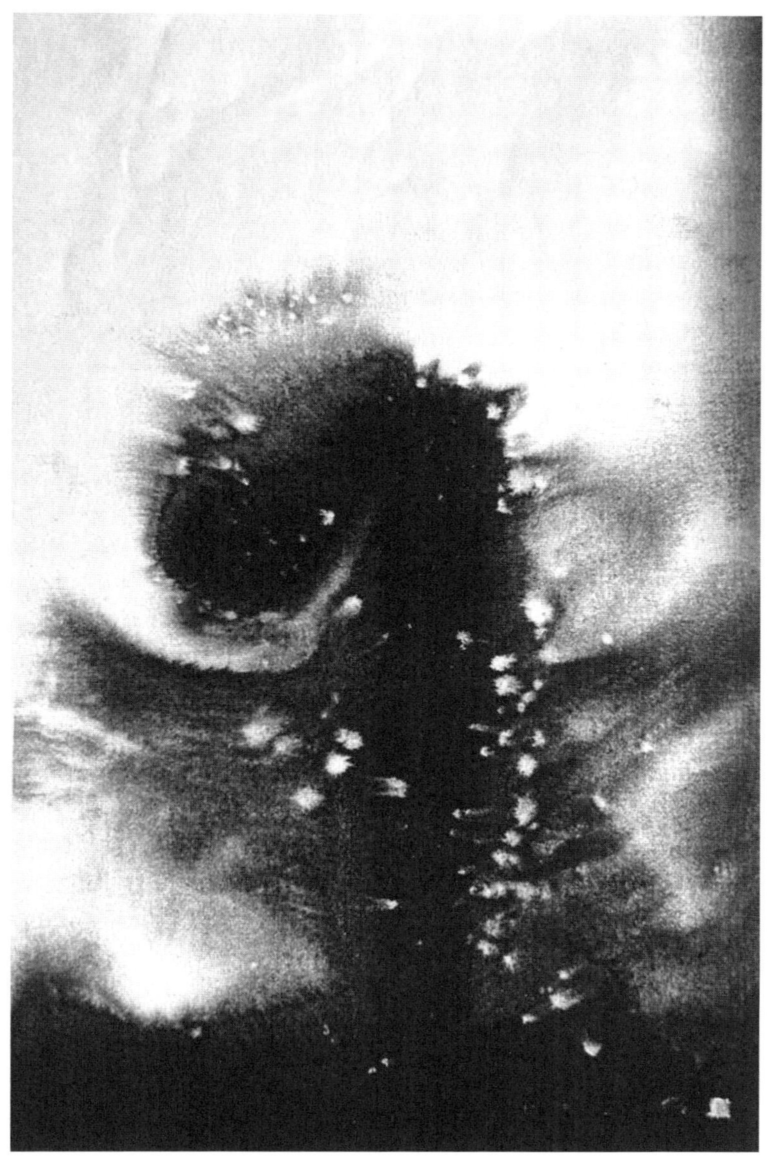

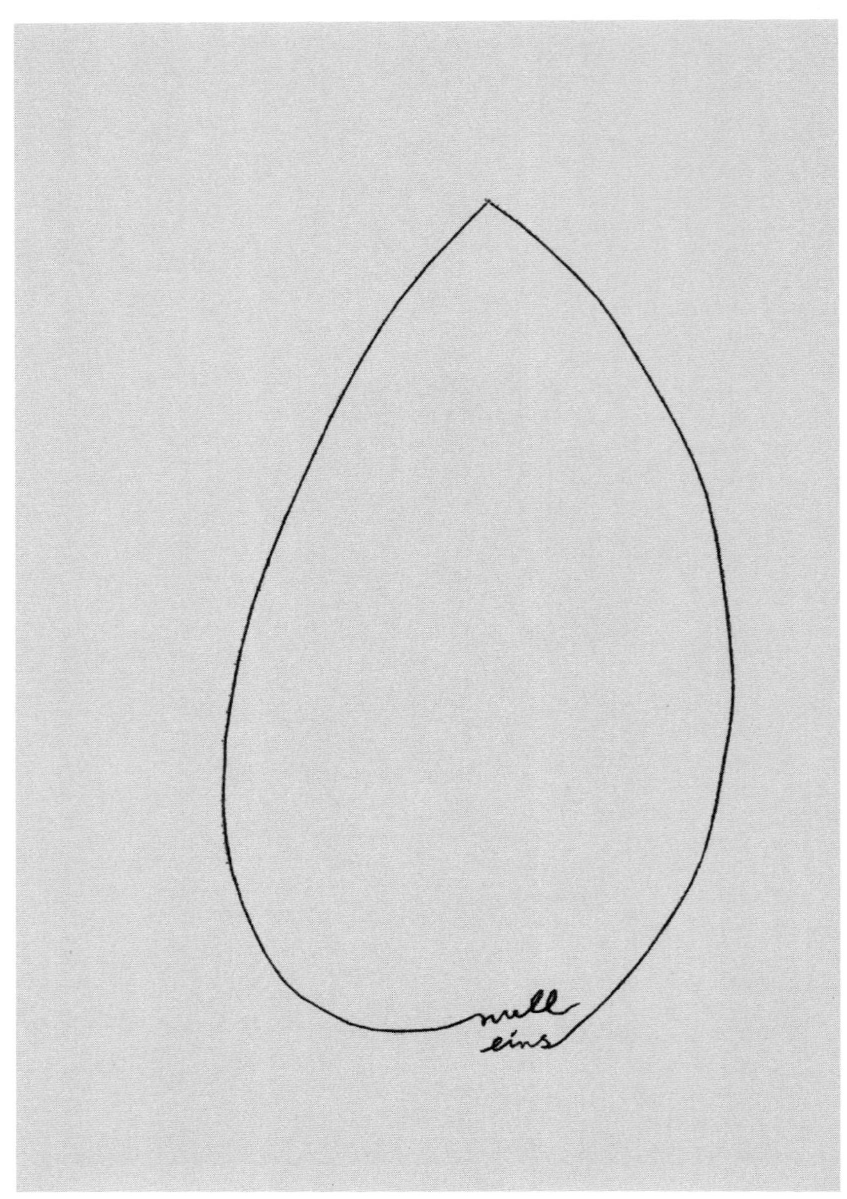

[null / eins = zero / one]

an eight that refuses to disintegrate

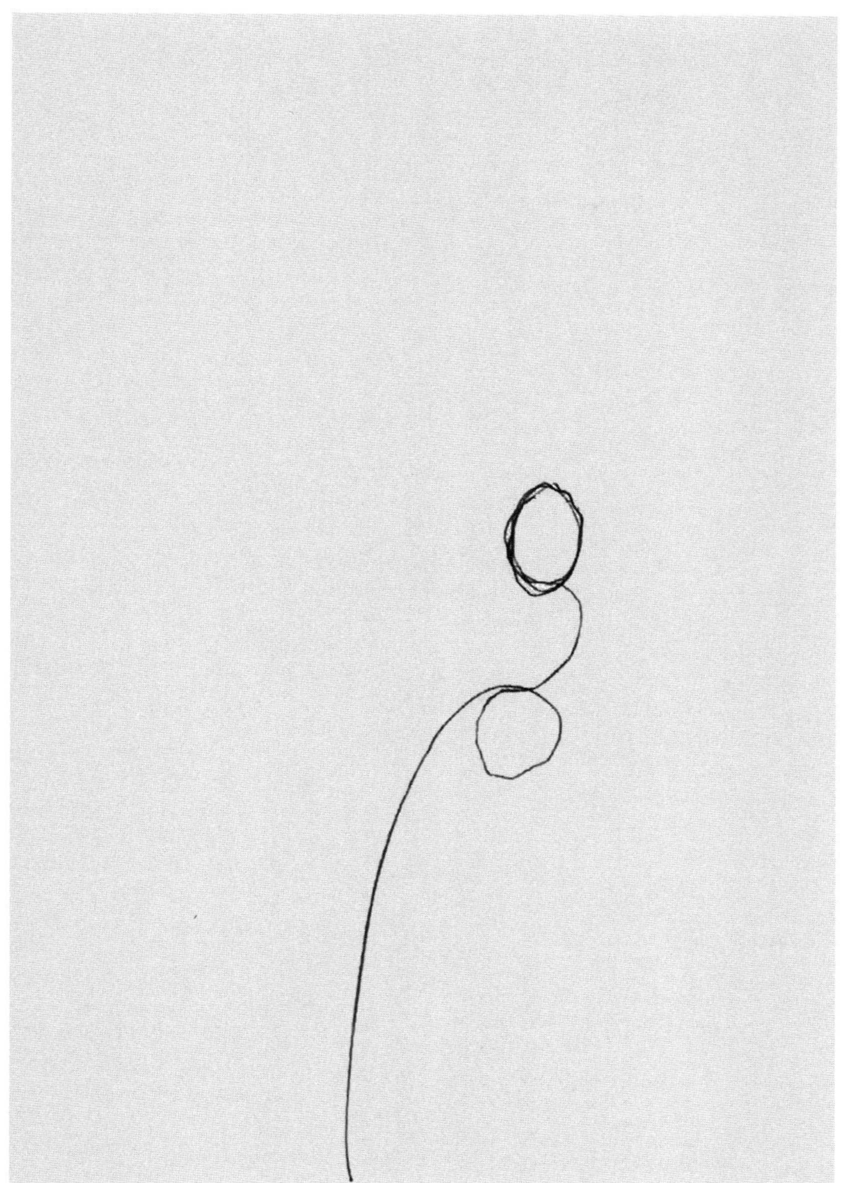

eight eights that refuse to disintegrate

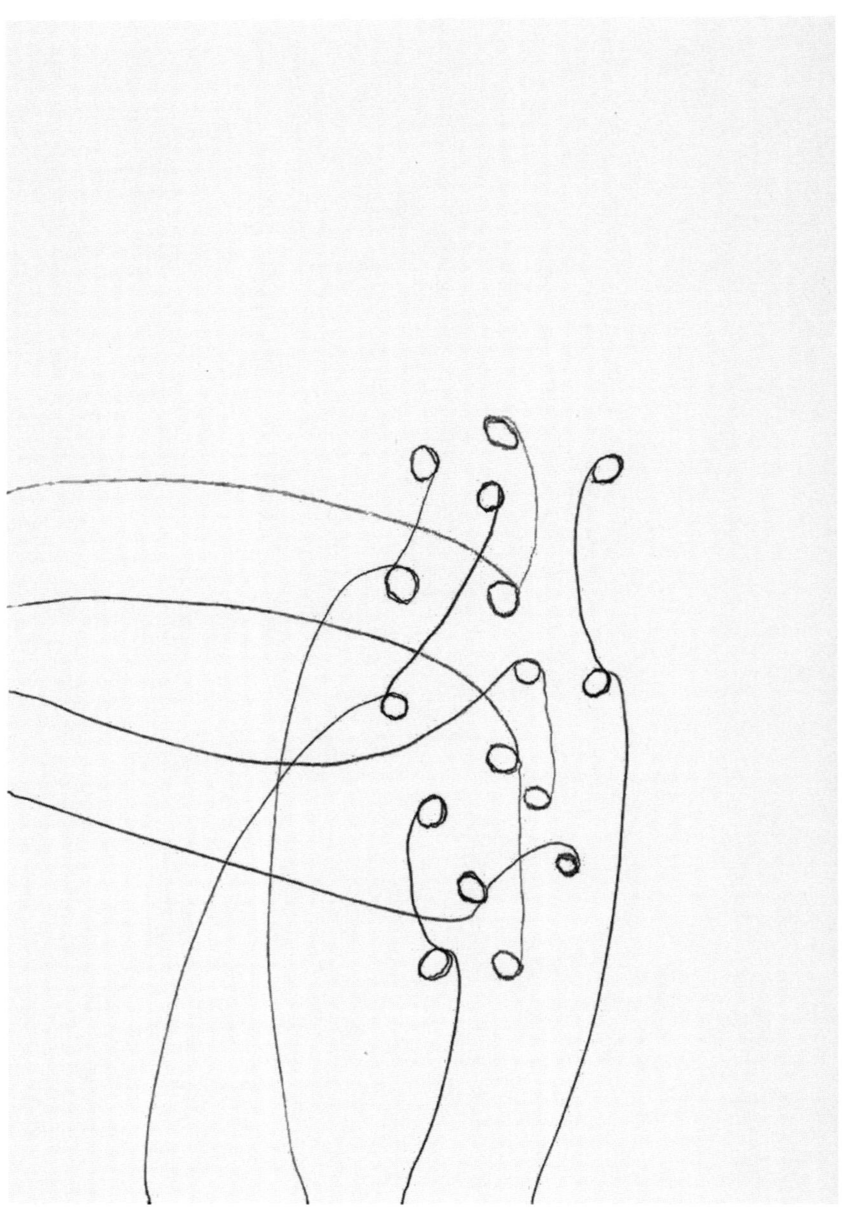

eight eights that must disintegrate

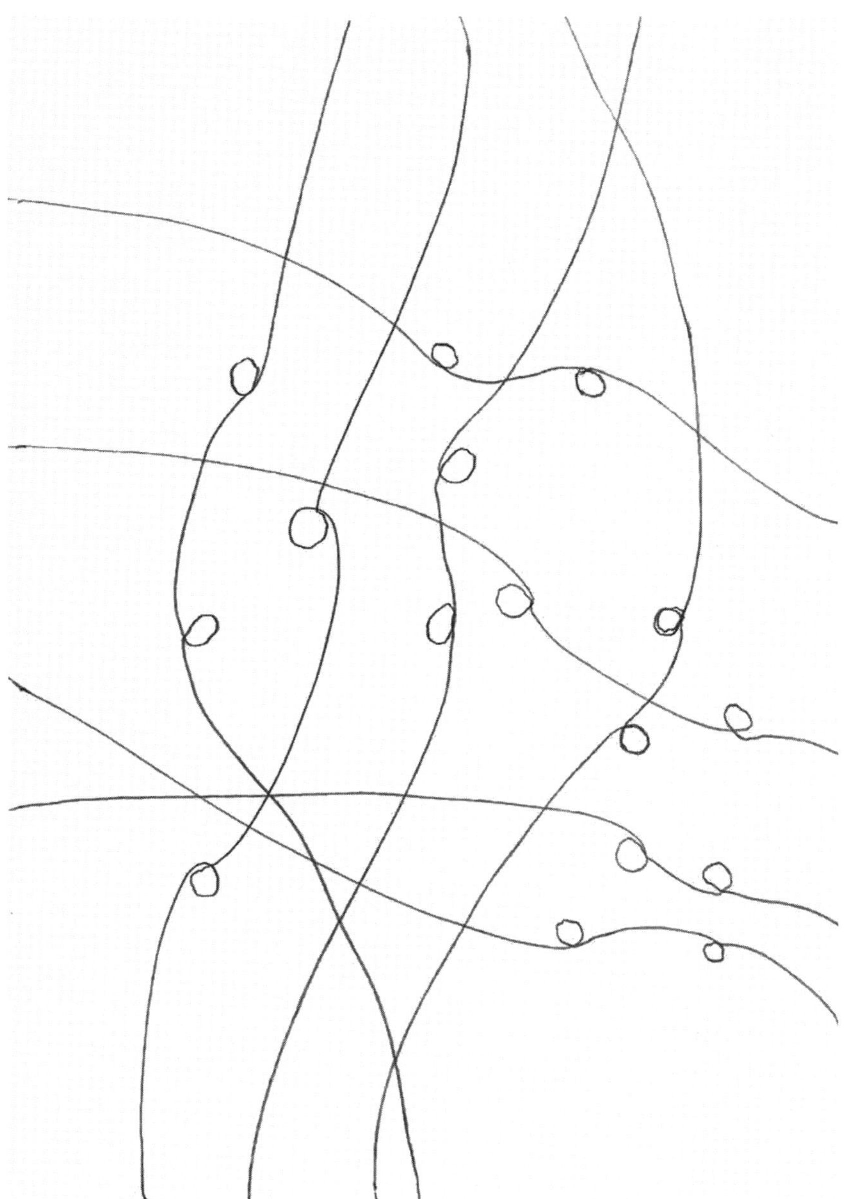

sunday protects its premature birth — saturday

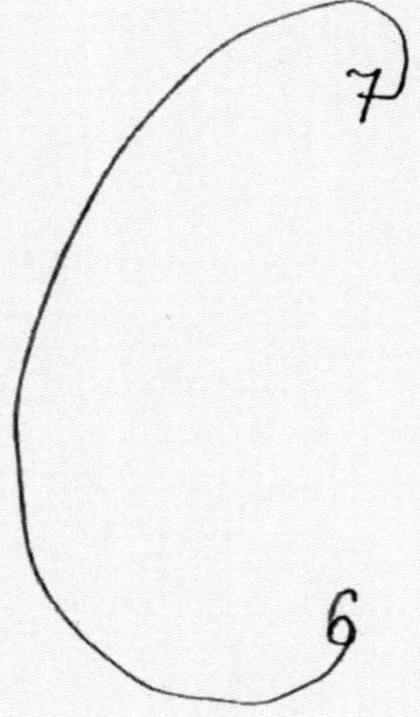

sunday attacks the first day of the week

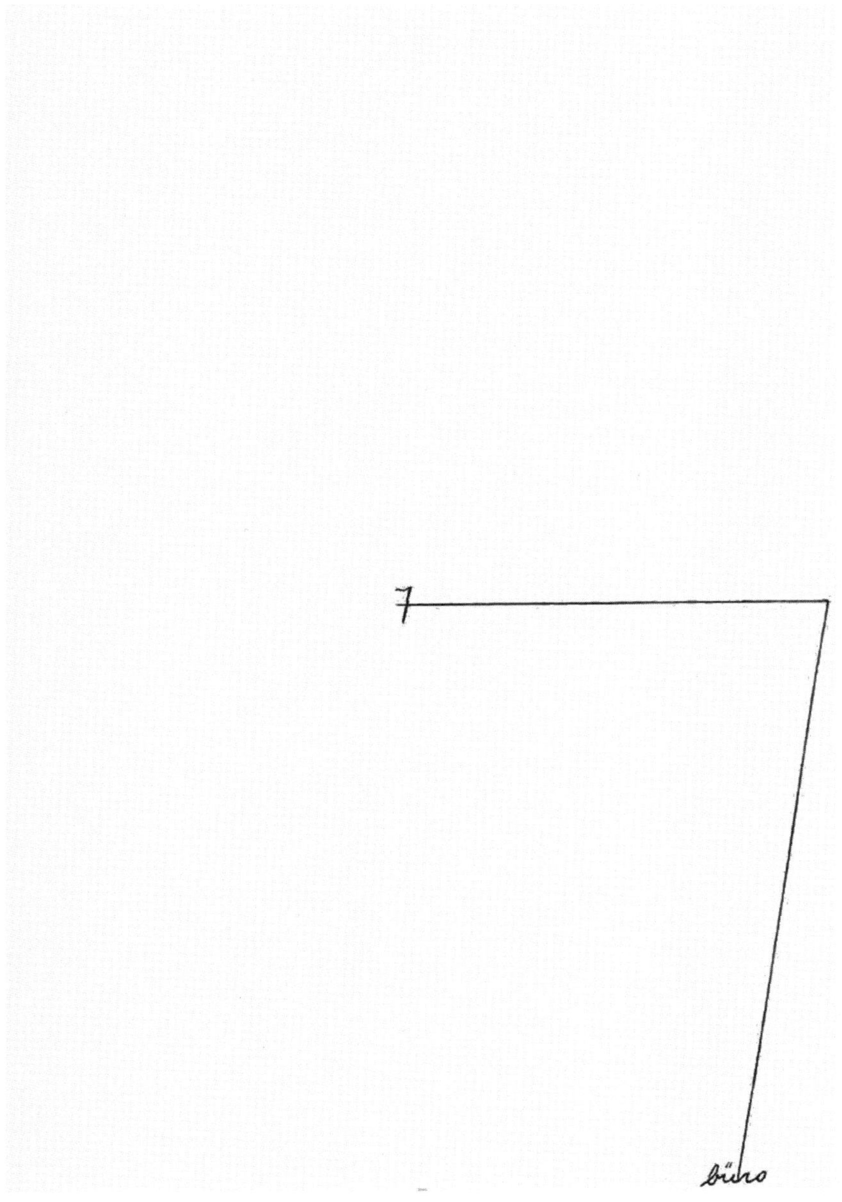

Qualitätsprüfung
durchgeführt von
Qualitätskontrolle

Nr. 22

vita

a note on recitation
from "exit" on, the recitation can be accompanied by incidental music. suggestions: the sounds of a busy street, the howling wind or a recording of miles davis's "in a silent way," 2nd half. after "all grown" a long pause.

entrance
one centimeter
two centimeters
three centimeters
four centimeters
five centimeters
six centimeters
seven centimeters
eight centimeters
nine centimeters
ten centimeters
eleven centimeters
twelve centimeters
thirteen centimeters
fourteen centimeters
fifteen centimeters
sixteen centimeters
seventeen centimeters
eighteen centimeters
nineteen centimeters
twenty centimeters
twenty-one centimeters
twenty-two centimeters

twenty-three centimeters
twenty-four centimeters
twenty-five centimeters
twenty-six centimeters
twenty-seven centimeters
twenty-eight centimeters
twenty-nine centimeters
thirty centimeters
thirty-one centimeters
thirty-two centimeters
thirty-three centimeters
thirty-four centimeters
thirty-five centimeters
thirty-six centimeters
thirty-seven centimeters
thirty-eight centimeters
thirty-nine centimeters
forty centimeters
forty-one centimeters
forty-two centimeters
forty-three centimeters
forty-four centimeters
forty-five centimeters
forty-six centimeters
forty-seven centimeters
forty-eight centimeters
forty-nine centimeters
fifty centimeters
fifty-one centimeters
fifty-two centimeters
fifty-three centimeters
fifty-four centimeters
fifty-five centimeters

fifty-six centimeters
fifty-seven centimeters
fifty-eight centimeters
fifty-nine centimeters
sixty centimeters
sixty-one centimeters
sixty-two centimeters
sixty-three centimeters
sixty-four centimeters
sixty-five centimeters
sixty-six centimeters
sixty-seven centimeters
sixty-eight centimeters
sixty-nine centimeters
seventy centimeters
seventy-one centimeters
seventy-two centimeters
seventy-three centimeters
seventy-four centimeters
seventy-five centimeters
seventy-six centimeters
seventy-seven centimeters
seventy-eight centimeters
seventy-nine centimeters
eighty centimeters
eighty-one centimeters
eighty-two centimeters
eighty-three centimeters
eighty-four centimeters
eighty-five centimeters
eighty-six centimeters
eighty-seven centimeters
eighty-eight centimeters

eighty-nine centimeters
ninety centimeters
ninety-one centimeters
ninety-two centimeters
ninety-three centimeters
ninety-four centimeters
ninety-five centimeters
ninety-six centimeters
ninety-seven centimeters
ninety-eight centimeters
ninety-nine centimeters
one hundred centimeters
one hundred one centimeters
one hundred two centimeters
one hundred three centimeters
one hundred four centimeters
one hundred five centimeters
one hundred six centimeters
one hundred seven centimeters
one hundred eight centimeters
one hundred nine centimeters
one hundred ten centimeters
one hundred eleven centimeters
one hundred twelve centimeters
one hundred thirteen centimeters
one hundred fourteen centimeters
one hundred fifteen centimeters
one hundred sixteen centimeters
one hundred seventeen centimeters
one hundred eighteen centimeters
one hundred nineteen centimeters
one hundred twenty centimeters
one hundred twenty-one centimeters

one hundred twenty-two centimeters
one hundred twenty-three centimeters
one hundred twenty-four centimeters
one hundred twenty-five centimeters
one hundred twenty-six centimeters
one hundred twenty-seven centimeters
one hundred twenty-eight centimeters
one hundred twenty-nine centimeters
one hundred thirty centimeters
one hundred thirty-one centimeters
one hundred thirty-two centimeters
one hundred thirty-three centimeters
one hundred thirty-four centimeters
one hundred thirty-five centimeters
one hundred thirty-six centimeters
one hundred thirty-seven centimeters
one hundred thirty-eight centimeters
one hundred thirty-nine centimeters
one hundred forty centimeters
one hundred forty-one centimeters
one hundred forty-two centimeters
one hundred forty-three centimeters
one hundred forty-four centimeters
one hundred forty-five centimeters
one hundred forty-six centimeters
one hundred forty-seven centimeters
one hundred forty-eight centimeters
one hundred forty-nine centimeters
one hundred fifty centimeters
one hundred fifty-one centimeters
one hundred fifty-two centimeters
one hundred fifty-three centimeters
one hundred fifty-four centimeters

one hundred fifty-five centimeters
one hundred fifty-six centimeters
one hundred fifty-seven centimeters
one hundred fifty-eight centimeters
one hundred fifty-nine centimeters
one hundred sixty centimeters
one hundred sixty-one centimeters
one hundred sixty-two centimeters
one hundred sixty-three centimeters
one hundred sixty-four centimeters
one hundred sixty-five centimeters
one hundred sixty-six centimeters
one hundred sixty-seven centimeters
one hundred sixty-eight centimeters
one hundred sixty-nine centimeters
one hundred seventy centimeters
one hundred seventy-one centimeters
one hundred seventy-two centimeters
one hundred seventy-three centimeters
one hundred seventy-four centimeters
one hundred seventy-five centimeters
all grown one hundred seventy-four centimeters
one hundred seventy-three centimeters
one hundred seventy-two centimeters
one hundred seventy-one centimeters
one hundred seventy centimeters
exit

a patchy row of numerals

. 2 . . . . 7 . . 10 . . . . . 16 17 18 19 . 21 22 23 24 25 26

in memoriam

from 1 to 26 & on into the infinite

1

2 2

3 3 3

4 4 4 4

5 5 5 5 5

6 6 6 6 6 6

7 7 7 7 7 7 7

8 8 8 8 8 8 8 8

9 9 9 9 9 9 9 9 9

10 10 10 10 10 10 10 10 10 10

11 11 11 11 11 11 11 11 11 11 11

12 12 12 12 12 12 12 12 12 12 12 12

13 13 13 13 13 13 13 13 13 13 13 13 13

14 14 14 14 14 14 14 14 14 14 14 14 14 14

15 15 15 15 15 15 15 15 15 15 15 15 15 15 15

16 16 16 16 16 16 16 16 16 16 16 16 16 16 16 16

17 17 17 17 17 17 17 17 17 17 17 17 17 17 17 17 17

18 18 18 18 18 18 18 18 18 18 18 18 18 18 18 18 18 18

19 19 19 19 19 19 19 19 19 19 19 19 19 19 19 19 19 19 19

20 20 20 20 20 20 20 20 20 20 20 20 20 20 20 20 20 20 20 20

21 21 21 21 21 21 21 21 21 21 21 21 21 21 21 21 21 21 21 21 21

22 22 22 22 22 22 22 22 22 22 22 22 22 22 22 22 22 22 22 22 22 22

23 23 23 23 23 23 23 23 23 23 23 23 23 23 23 23 23 23 23 23 23 23 23

24 24 24 24 24 24 24 24 24 24 24 24 24 24 24 24 24 24 24 24 24 24 24 24

25 25 25 25 25 25 25 25 25 25 25 25 25 25 25 25 25 25 25 25 25 25 25 25 25

26 26 26 26 26 26 26 26 26 26 26 26 26 26 26 26 26 26 26 26 26 26 26 26 26 26

etc.

beyond the sheet of paper, beyond the table, beyond the room, beyond the house, beyond the street, the city, the country, beyond the whole wide world, the solar system, beyond the milky way, and on, further and further away . . .

the folded clock

twelve possibilities
something has changed

eleven possibilities
shades of blue

something has changed
ten possibilities

for the first time
shades of blue

something has changed
nine possibilities

unexpected
for the second time

shades of blue
something has changed

eight possibilities
the universe expands

expected and unexpected
for the third time

shades of blue
something has changed

seven possibilities
gray in gray

the universe expands
expected and and unexpected

for the fourth time
shades of blue

something has changed
six possibilities

yes or no
gray in gray

the universe expands
expected and and and unexpected

for the fifth time
shades of blue

something has changed
five possibilities

one of us turns on the light when it gets dark
yes or no

gray in gray
the universe expands

expected and and and and unexpected
for the sixth time

shades of blue
something has changed

four possibilities
a reunion

one of us turns on the light when it gets dark
yes or no

gray in gray
the universe expands

expected and and and and and unexpected
for the seventh time

shades of blue
something has changed

three possibilities
found imagined

a reunion
one of us turns on the light when it gets dark

yes or no
gray in gray

the universe expands
expected and and and and and and unexpected

for the eighth time
shades of blue

something has changed
two possibilities

carrying on together
found imagined

a reunion
one of us turns on the light when it gets dark

yes or no
gray in gray

the universe expands
expected and and and and and and and unexpected

for the ninth time
shades of blue

something has changed
one possibility

something is changing
shades of blue

for the tenth time
expected and and and and and and and and unexpected

the universe expands
gray in gray

yes
one of us turns on the light when it gets dark

the reunion
found imagined

carrying on together
shades of blue

for the eleventh time
expected and and and and and and and and and unexpected

the universe expands
gray in gray

yes
one of us turns on the light when it gets dark

the reunion
found imagined

carrying on together
for the twelfth time

expected and and and and and and and and and and unexpected
the universe expands

gray in gray
yes or no

found imagined
carrying on together

expected and and and and and and and and and and and unexpected
the universe expands

gray in gray
yes or no

one of us turns on the light when it gets dark
the reunion

found imagined
carrying on together

the universe expands
gray in gray

yes
one of us turns on the light when it gets dark

the reunion
found imagined

carrying on together
gray in gray

yes
one of us turns on the light when it gets dark

the reunion
found imagined

carrying on together
yes

one of us turns on the light when it gets dark
the reunion

found imagined
carrying on together

one of us turns on the light when it gets dark
the reunion

found imagined
carrying on together

the reunion
found imagined

carrying on together
found imagined

carrying on together
carrying on together

postscript

the number, at least as far as structure goes, is the common denominator of all the sundry forms of art, as well as of all measurable forms of appearance in general. everything visible and audible — insofar as not the carrier of a sign, i.e., without any additional semantic function to fulfill — can be traced back to purely numerical relationships and can therefore also be translated from one dimension to another. musical ideas can be adequately notated graphically — much more precisely than traditional musical notation. conversely, graphic structures can be translated into tonal structures — "graphic notation" has thematized this very possibility. it is now perfectly reasonable to simply limit ourselves to the presentation of pure numerical relationships, in other words, to dispense with musical or artistic form altogether. without being aware of kurt schwitters' number poems, i wrote my first number poem in 1954. since then i have repeatedly returned to the number as the most pared-down and at the same time most universal element of design.

on individual texts

"a recounting" (p. 13) is also available in a film version produced by saarländisches television with me as the director, narrator and actor.

i regard "101. a number poem" (p. 19), written in the early 1960s, to be a work of prose whose "plot" has to do with constant new attempts to arrive at the number given in the title, 101. as this fails, the attempt is forcibly brought to a standstill by the gradual superimposition of new basic numbers.

the four image texts on pp. 60 to 63 are typewriter ideograms on a4 sheets of paper that had to be reduced to book size, which was unavoidable with some of the other image texts as well.

if on pages 69 and 70 the *eins* is pronounced with the *m* directly in front of it and in the second case the *eins* with the *t* after it, the impression, which may initially seem perplexing, will quickly become obvious.

"definitive" (p. 93) is a slightly corrected version of a poem published in my collection *epigrams and epitaphs*.
"an austrian counting poem" (p. 103) is based on documented statements made by a well-known austrian people's party (ÖVP) politician. as incredible and barbaric as it may be, the politician was not punished in any way. it is typical of the political morality of austria that the minister did not have to resign immediately but was allowed to continue in office with no restrictions whatsoever.
the "birthday party" (p. 110) refers to a newspaper report of an actual incident.
"a bruckner anecdote" (p. 115) refers to anton bruckner's mania for numbers. it is said that on numerous occasions he had to compulsively count facts and things. this is a monovocal repetition study attributed to him.
"auction of a cracker from the 'titanic'" (p. 125) also refers to an actual incident.
"a patchy row of numerals" (p. 163) has something to do with the kabbalah insofar as the alphabet is assigned a sequence of numbers from one up, which allows coded combinations of numbers to be translated back into words.

gerhard rühm

GERHARD RÜHM was born in Vienna, Austria, in 1930. A writer, composer, and visual artist, he is truly one of the key figures of the postwar European avant-garde. With his earliest work dating to the late 1940s, he was one of the first practitioners of concrete poetry and a founding member of the legendary Wiener Gruppe in the 1950s. His lifelong study of music has had a lasting impact on his multifaceted work with its amalgams of music and language and image and text. The result has been a decades-long exploration of a broad range of forms — poetry, prose, radio plays, drama scenarios, musical compositions, visual compositions, collages, and graphic art — drawing on a lineage that can be traced to Dadaism, Surrealism, and Dark Romanticism. His more recent work cleverly incorporates pornographic motifs while skewering the Church and regularly invoking the aesthetics of ugliness, vulgarity, and banality. Rühm has received numerous awards, including the Austrian State Prize in 1991 and the America Award in Literature in 2022. He currently divides his time between Cologne and Vienna.

ALEXANDER BOOTH, originally from Virginia, is a poet, translator, collage artist, and printmaker who lives in Berlin. The recipient of support from the German Translators' Fund and PEN America, his translations from German include work by Friederike Mayröcker, Alexander Kluge, Jürgen Becker, Lutz Seiler, and a new translation of Ludwig Wittgenstein's *Tractatus Logico-Philosophicus.*

the folded clock: 100 number poems by Gerhard Rühm
is translated by Alexander Booth
from the original German *die gefaltete uhr. 100 zahlendichtungen*
(Klagenfurt, Graz und Wien: Ritter Verlag, 2023)

All images by Gerhard Rühm

Book designed and set in Futura PT by Silk Mountain

Printed and bound in the Czech Republic by TISKÁRNA PROTISK

FIRST EDITION 2025

Twisted Spoon Press
P.O. Box 21 — Preslova 12
150 00 Prague 5
Czech Republic
www.twistedspoon.com

TRADE DISTRIBUTION :
CENTRAL BOOKS
www.centralbooks.com

SCB DISTRIBUTORS
www.scbdistributors.com